ENDING LIVES

ROBERT CAMPBELL
DIANÉ COLLINSON

Basil Blackwell
in association with
the Open University

First published 1988
Reprinted 1988, 1991

Basil Blackwell Ltd
108 Cowley Road, Oxford, OX4 1JF, UK

Basil Blackwell Inc.
3 Cambridge Center
Cambridge, Massachusetts 02142, USA

British Library Cataloguing in Publication Data
Campbell, Robert
  Ending lives
  1. Euthanasia—Moral and ethical aspects
  2. Suicide
  I. Title   II. Collinson, Diané   III. Open University
  174′24   R726

  ISBN 0–631–15329–2
  ISBN 0–631–15331–4   pbk

Library of Congress Cataloging in Publication Data
Campbell, Robert
  Ending lives/Robert Campbell and Diané Collinson
  p. cm.
  Includes index
  ISBN 0–631–15329–2 (U.S.)   ISBN 0–631–15331–4 (pbk.)
  1. Suicide   2. Euthanasia   I. Collinson, Diané, 1930–
  II. Title
  BD445.C36 1988
  179′.7—dc19   87–29366   CIP

This book forms part of an Open University course, A310 *Life and Death*.
For further information about this course, please write to the
Student Enquiries Office, The Open University, PO Box 71,
Walton Hall, Milton Keynes, MK7 6AG, UK.

Typeset in 11 on 12½ pt Bembo
by Photo·graphics, Honiton, Devon
Printed in Great Britain by Billing & Sons Ltd, Worcester

Contents

Preface

This book is part of an Open University course in applied ethics called *Life and Death*.

The authors would like to thank Open University colleagues on the A310 *Life and Death* course team for comments on earlier drafts, but particularly Tom Sorell, course team chair, and Peter Wright, course editor. The authors are also grateful to the external reader of the book, Professor Anthony Manser, and the medical assessor, Dr Mary Lobjoit, who both made valuable comments throughout the draft stages. Thanks are also due to John Harris, the course assessor, for advice on he final draft.

Diané Collinson would like to record her gratitude to Dennis Collinson for his unfailing forbearance and generosity.

Robert Campbell would like to thank Bolton Institute of Higher Education for granting a term's secondment for work on the book, and also Lynn Campbell for her advice and support.

Although the authors collaborated throughout, Diané Collinson was principally responsible for Chapters One to Five and Robert Campbell for the Introduction and Chapters Six to Eight.

Introduction

Death is inevitable, but the time of death is increasingly under our control. Improvements in public health and medical technology mean that we can prolong life, sometimes beyond the point at which people want to continue to live. Can it be right to seek to end life before it is lost? Are there circumstances in which either suicide or euthanasia would be justified?

It is usually taken to be obvious that to kill someone is to harm them. Is it possible that someone could be benefited by death? We know that a person can be so driven by external circumstances or mental anguish that they attempt to commit suicide. We may think we understand how they could come to believe that death would be preferable to the life they had. It is quite another issue, however, whether they are right to think this way, whether what they did was rational and defensible. This comes out most clearly if we consider whether we would ever feel obliged to try to stop someone from committing suicide.

Euthanasia raises the same question. Ending someone's life painlessly would not normally be thought of as euthanasia unless there was some sense in which death would be a benefit to them. Certainly no 'euthanasia' which was not done for the good of the one who died could ever be desirable (though it may be necessary, see Chapter Eight 'Should the numbers count?').

Some consideration of why life is valuable and when and how it may cease to be of value to the one whose life it is, is essential to an examination of both suicide and euthanasia. This, in itself, would be a good reason for dealing with both in the same book. But there is, in addition, a relatively common and philosophically important class of cases where suicide and euthanasia overlap and merge together.

Let us imagine someone, 'A', who decides to commit suicide. He is no longer as young or as fit as he was, he has little to look forward to and, because most of his friends and all his close relatives are dead, no one to leave behind. Rather than live on into what he sees as an increasingly bleak and cheerless old age, he decides to end it all now. For this purpose he accumulates a supply of sleeping pills for which he has a regular prescription from his doctor and, when he judges he has enough, takes them all. He leaves a note explaining his action and the reasons for it.

A's action would seem to be suicide pure and simple. But suppose A's doctor suspects that she knows the reason why A keeps on requesting sleeping pills and, having considered what she should do, decides that in A's position she would do the same, that A's decision is perfectly reasonable and that, consequently, she has neither the right, nor the inclination, to interfere with it. Are we still dealing with suicide pure and simple, or is this suicide 'assisted'? From A's point of view it *is* suicide; from the point of view of a third party it begins to take on some of the characteristics of euthanasia, once the doctor's decision is taken into account.

If you do not feel that this makes the point sufficiently clearly, consider a similar, but slightly altered, version of the case. A, when he requests the sleeping pills, explains to the doctor what he wants them for and asks her advice about the correct dosage for his purpose. She gives it. Or again, imagine someone like A, except that he is bedridden and physically weak. He asks the doctor not just to supply the means for his suicide, but to administer it. Perhaps this is no longer a borderline case, but one which we would unhesitatingly call 'euthanasia'. But from the point of view of the patient it still is no different from suicide except in, for him, inessential respects.

The point is that by gradually altering details of the case

we can move almost imperceptibly from a case which is clearly suicide and nothing else, to one which is clearly euthanasia. Lord Kilbrandon, a Law Lord, once remarked, in talking of murder, that it seems pointless to let much hang on the distinction between the person who actually pulls the trigger, and the person who loads the gun and hands it to him, so long as both knew what they were doing, of course. The same seems to be true of suicide and euthanasia. Whether A kills himself unaided, or with assistance, or persuades someone else to do it for him hardly seems to matter from the point of view of whether A is justified in wanting to die and, given that he does want to, whether it is justifiable that he should die.

The same point can be made the other way round (though it very seldom is, which is both interesting and, perhaps, significant). It is often taken as self-evident that killing people is wrong. This, as we shall see, may be true, but is much too simplistic. Nonetheless, if it is true that killing people is wrong, why should it make a difference if the person you kill is yourself? On the face of it, if euthanasia is wrong because it involves killing someone, then suicide is wrong for exactly the same reason. Equally, if a particular suicide is not wrong, then how could it be that euthanasia in just such a case could be wrong?

There are good reasons, therefore, for wanting to examine suicide and euthanasia in sequence, both for the questions that they jointly raise and for the light that each can throw upon the other. What will not figure prominently in this book are religion, law and medicine. This may seem surprising. All three come up in what follows. Religious doctrines and theological arguments are analysed, medical cases and techniques are considered and some of the legal background is discussed. But this is not a theological, medical or a legal text. The problems are considered not from the perspective of any of these disciplines, but from a philosophical point of view. What does this imply, and what are the reasons for it?

We readily acknowledge the roles played by religion, medicine and the law in defining the problems we shall consider, but we do not see that they can, in themselves, contribute to solving them. Orthodox Roman Catholic doctrine, for example, declares that suicide is, normally, a sin and that euthanasia is wrong. Anglican and Judaic teaching is, with some variation, in agreement with this. For those who are not Catholics, Anglicans or Jews, this is only an interesting but inconclusive fact of the debate. Even for those who accept this doctrine on faith or on the authority of the Church, there are further questions to be asked about why this is the doctrine, what it is based on, whether it is always and absolutely binding, what kinds of case it applies to. These further questions are philosophical ones and since they call the religious viewpoint into question, religion cannot be used to answer them.

Equally medical knowledge and judgement is required to tell us, for example, what 'Down's syndrome' is, what it implies for those who suffer from it and what prognosis can be expected for them. A doctor cannot tell us, in virtue of what she knows *as a doctor*, whether those who suffer from Down's syndrome should always have medical treatment if their lives are threatened by illness or congenital defect. Doctors are normally aware of this, but the rest of us often expect them to answer what are not essentially medical questions, simply on the basis of their medical training and experience. Just because a treatment exists does not mean that we should use it and, as we shall see, justice and charity (though *not* medical science) may, on occasion, require us not to use it.

A similar point can be made about the law. It is not neutral. It embodies the moral values and concepts of generations of law-makers and can also be used as an instrument of social policy by governments. Knowing what the law is, therefore, is not the same as knowing what it ought to be. Even determining what the law is is not always an exclusively legal exercise. Much law is couched in terms of ordinary moral concepts like 'honesty', 'malice', 'duty' and 'care'. The law, in effect, relies on us to supply a moral content to its enactments and judgements so that we cannot appeal to the law without at the same time considering what morality demands and prescribes.

Doctors, lawyers and theologians cannot, simply in view

of their special knowledge and training, give us answers to the questions we face. Neither, it must be said, can philosophers. What philosophy can do is to focus on what is essential and what is not, in a particular situation; to remind us, by analogy and example, of what we already think and to point out inconsistencies and incoherences in our views. Sometimes, though not very often, this is sufficient to resolve our problems. Even where it is not, however, it does enable us to determine what really matters to us and what we have to confront in order to secure it. We are not, therefore, claiming that philosophy has a superior position in the hierarchy of knowledge. Still less would we maintain that this book makes all the theological, medical and legal work done on these topics superfluous. But philosophy does have an essential and distinctive contribution to make to the debate and *Ending Lives*, we hope, can properly sit alongside the medical and legal texts and theological expositions that have dealt with suicide and euthanasia.

Most of us would agree that killing people is wrong. Murder is usually held to be the most serious – though not necessarily always the nastiest – category of crime that the law recognizes, and it seems to be true that a strong inhibition against killing members of the same species is built into most higher animals. Nonetheless there are exceptions to this. All, except pacifists, would acknowledge that in times of war it is often necessary to kill combatants on the opposing side. Equally most people would allow that self-defence permits you to do what you have to do to protect yourself from a serious threat of harm, up to and including killing your attacker. A policeman may justifiably shoot an armed terrorist who, despite being warned, continues to threaten to kill innocent bystanders. We could continue this list for some time and, although not everyone would agree that all of these were justifiable exceptions to the principle that killing people is wrong, nearly everyone would agree that there are exceptions of this kind. This need not be an inconsistent view to take. Why is killing people wrong? One answer might be that human life has value and that to kill a human being is to destroy that value. But if there are situations where it is necessary to kill some people in order to save the lives of others, then the same principle, that human life has value, could be appealed to in order to justify killing.

This kind of appeal is often heard in defence of the decision made by the Allied Forces towards the end of the Second World War, to drop atom bombs on Hiroshima and Nagasaki. It was fully realized that doing so would cost enormous numbers of Japanese lives. Most of these were non-combatants and civilians, but it was felt that only in this way could the Japanese be induced to surrender. The 'honour' code of the Japanese made surrender a shameful thing, so it was feared that in the face of more conventional military tactics, they would continue to wage war until totally and completely defeated. This would, it was estimated, cost many thousands of lives, both Allied and Japanese, and prolong the war by months or even years. The death toll which followed the dropping of the atom bombs needed, therefore, to be measured against what was thought to be a much greater number of lives that would be lost were the Japanese not to surrender. The appeal is, in other words, to the number of lives *saved* as a result of the killing. The appeal carries no conviction, of course, unless more lives are saved than are lost.

Similarly the justification for killing in self-defence could be made out in terms of the necessity to kill in order to save life. Though there is normally no benefit here in terms of numbers of lives saved, self-defence killings are thought to be justified because the victim is innocent and the aggressor, in virtue of the attack, has made herself guilty. This is plausible because self-defence killings are only justifiable in response to a credible and immediate threat to life. You may not, in the United Kingdom, kill a burglar in defence of the family jewels, and though in the United States you could be acquitted in such a case, this is probably due to the greater likelihood in the United States of the burglar being armed and prepared to kill if disturbed. Equally you cannot kill someone who has merely threatened that they will, at some future time, attack you, because there are presumably ways other than by killing of averting the threat.

One argument, though not the only one, for capital punishment, follows similar lines. Taking life through judicial execution is a terrible thing, but we must think not only of the loss of the criminal's life, but also of potential future victims. Perhaps this particular criminal will not murder again because, for example, she has been given life imprisonment. But the lack of a death penalty may mean that other would-be murderers are not deterred from their crimes. Capital punishment, on the other hand, might deter them and thus, although murderers are executed and human lives are lost thereby, many more potential murderers are deterred and the lives of their contemplated victims are saved.

At this stage we need to ask not whether these conclusions are true, but whether the arguments given in support of them are valid. We are not concerned, at the moment, with whether capital punishment or the use of nuclear weapons can ever be morally justified, but with what kind of argument is being deployed in their defence. We must leave to one side the factual, though far from straightforward, questions of whether dropping the atom bomb on Hiroshima and Nagasaki did save more lives than it cost, or whether capital punishment really is a deterrent to crimes of murder. But if the answer to both were 'yes', would it follow that the use of the atom bomb and the institution of capital punishment were justified? If it is also true that acting so as to save more human lives is better than acting to save fewer because human life has value, then it seems it would.

We began with a moral principle – killing people is wrong – which we suggested most people would accept. We then pointed out that many of the same people would also accept that there are, apparently, exceptions to this principle. We then suggested that there is a higher principle – that we must act so as to save as many human lives as possible – which explained both our first principle and also the apparent exceptions. Does this higher principle have exceptions? If suicide and euthanasia are ever justified, then there would be. For it is rare that acts of suicide or euthanasia actually save more lives than they cost. We may think of the case of Captain Oates, who walked out into a polar storm with the intention of dying and thereby increasing his companions' chances of survival. Nomadic Eskimo tribes used to abandon aged and infirm members of the tribe to die because to try and care for them might endanger the lives of the whole tribe. Such examples are comparatively rare and some would argue that Oates is not actually an example of true suicide (see Chapter One 'The nature of suicide'). More usually neither suicide nor euthanasia results in more lives being saved than lost (though in regard to euthanasia, see Chapter Eight 'Should the numbers count?'). So neither could be justified by appeal to the higher principle we have identified.

We have two options in the face of this. One is to conclude that suicide and euthanasia are not justified except where they are aimed at saving lives in the long run. This seems an implausible conclusion to draw; it is certainly counter-intuitive in the sense that most people's moral convictions would be that there may be cases of justifiable suicide or euthanasia which were not, and were not intended to be, likely to save lives, on balance, rather than lose them. The second option, then, is to assume that it is at least possible that cases of justifiable suicide and euthanasia exist and to try and reconcile that assumption with the belief that human life has value and that, other things being equal, one must seek to preserve it whenever one can. It is this second option that *Ending Lives* seeks to explore.

Despite the common ground which exists between suicide and euthanasia, there are clear differences between them and the most obvious difference is also the most important. Suicide is the only form of killing where the killer and the one killed are the same person. One very common view of morality is that essentially it involves our relationships with others. What we do by and to ourselves, so long as it harms no one else, is no one else's business. On this view there is no moral problem of suicide at all, apart from the effect our suicide may have on the duties and responsibilities we owe to others.

There is a tension between this view – that suicide *as such* is not a moral issue – and the one we have discussed – that human life must be preserved wherever possible. Out of this tension is created the problem of suicide, though the tension itself does not explain one feature of many people's reactions to the idea of suicide. For many suicide is a *special* kind of moral wrong, not necessarily the worst kind, but distinctive in its wrongness. This point emerges from the discussion of the nature of suicide in Chapter One. In an attempt to explain why we feel this way about suicide and to relate the feeling to other components of the concept of suicide, the history of the debate about suicide is examined in Chapter Two. For our attitude to suicide has shifted significantly through time and, it is suggested, this is connected to the way in which our attitude to the nature and value of human life has shifted. This point is explored further in Chapter Three where a particular view about human existence – that it is absurd or meaningless – is shown to raise the issue of suicide in a rather striking way. From this viewpoint suicide is less a moral issue than a metaphysical one, because the question of why one should continue to live a life which, on a cosmic scale, has neither value nor significance, is one which precedes all other philosophical questions. Chapter Four looks at existentialism which, especially in the hands of Sartre, argues that we create ourselves through our choices. The freedom this faces us with is terrifying and most prefer to deny it by pretending that it does not exist. The importance of suicide lies in the way it forces us to acknowledge that the ultimate choice – that of not existing – is always open to us and that in continuing to live we affirm, and are responsible for affirming, the value of life. The suicide denies that value through her suicide and thus her action threatens us in a particularly fundamental way.

Existentialism is not beyond criticism. In particular the idea that all choice is entirely unconstrained and beyond rationality seems implausible. But the idea of a close connection between what we choose and what we are seems worth preserving. In Chapter 5 the implications of this idea are examined. If we, as moral agents, are responsible for creating ourselves as the persons we are, then the idea of suicide will, paradoxically, be both an assertion of that responsibility and an abnegation of it. It is this which makes the idea of suicide such a terrible one to contemplate. Nonetheless, because it is imaginable that we may, through circumstances, find our moral choices so constricted or pointless that they no longer hold any meaning for us, the idea of suicide cannot entirely be ruled out.

Chapter Six, accordingly, examines the question of when it may or may not be permitted to end life. It argues that at least one class of cases often cited in support of the permissibility of euthanasia is not, properly, euthanasia at all. Letting someone die when there is little prospect of prolonging meaningful life for them is not to end their life, but to acknowledge that it is already, or shortly to be, ended.

Chapter Seven looks at an alternative distinction to that between killing and letting die, and suggests that it is more fruitful to distinguish between intending death, and foreseeing but not intending death. This is not a new distinction, but one which has been much criticized recently, and it is defended here. Chapter Seven concludes by considering some cases where genuine euthanasia may be morally permissible.

Distributing health care resources justly raises the question of whether we may ever sacrifice some lives in order to save others (see p. xiv and what follows, above). In Chapter Eight the conclusions drawn from the discussions about suicide are used to argue that, although we may quite properly choose to put our resources where they will save most lives, we may not *use* the death of some in order to benefit others, no matter what the numbers involved may be.

CHAPTER ONE

The nature of suicide

1 CONCEPTUAL DISTINCTIONS

'Those who commit suicide kill themselves.' Yes: but of course, that does not mean that all self-killings are suicide. If, for example, I inadvertently electrocute myself in amateurishly attempting to repair a piece of electrical equipment, or if I die as the result of diving from a height into a shallow pool that I thought was deep, then I certainly may be said to have killed myself but to have done so accidentally, not suicidally.

The statement about suicide must therefore have added to it something to the effect that suicide is a deliberate or intentional self-killing. But 'deliberate', one quickly realizes, will not entirely do because it implies reflective premeditation and so cannot cover self-killings that are impetuous and unpremeditated but that are nevertheless regarded as suicides. We have, therefore, to try 'intentional self-killing' as a description of suicide. This is to invoke a concept of considerable philosophical and moral resonance – that of intention – and I think its invocation will sharpen our understanding of the nature of suicide.

Central and unequivocal cases of suicide are those in which the intention with which suicide is committed is simply the intention to be dead: a person weary of life through pain or misery resolves to cease living and the act of self-killing is then the realization of that intention to be dead. But sometimes the intention with which a life is ended is one that is further to the actual self-killing: a man injured while taking part in a Himalayan climbing expedition, for example, may kill himself with the intention of enabling the other climbers to continue and succeed in their venture. In the first case – that of a person weary of life – death is what is aimed at. In the second case – that of the injured climber – death is a means of achieving or is instrumental to some other aim. And there does seem to be at least one further kind of suicide: suicide that is committed not so much with the intention of being dead or of realizing some aim to which the self-killing is a means, as purely for the sake of performing the act of killing oneself. In such·cases death itself seems to be less significant than the actual act of self-slaughter. The artistic movement known as Dadaism[1] that was widespread in Europe from about 1916 to 1924 produced a number of such deaths. The Japanese ritual suicide, seppuku,[2] better known as hara-kiri, seems to have this element in it. Although seppuku was often commanded as a punishment it was also a mode of honourable self-assertion and self-vindication in which every move in the ritual disembowelling and self-slaughter was significant.

2   INTENTION

The distinction between the accidental and the intentional requires further elaboration. An accidental occurrence is something one has not planned or foreseen; it happens rather than is brought about, or it is something that is involuntary in that we do not know we are bringing it about or do not mean to bring it about. In contrast, an intentional action is one that the agent means to do, voluntarily and knowingly. It expresses something about the agent. When we know the intention with which someone acts we know both the point of the action and something about the person who acts. When we know the intention with which an arm, for example, is raised, we then know what the person who raises an arm is doing: casting a vote, perhaps, or greeting a friend, dispelling insects, giving the signal to start a revolution or, like Stevie Smith's bather, 'not waving but drowning'.[3]

These theoretical or conceptual distinctions between the accidental and the intentional can be arrived at without a great deal of difficulty. But the business of establishing in a particular case what in fact is intentional and what accidental is not so straightforward. It is, for example, often maintained that some cases of apparently accidental self-killing are in fact manifestations of a suicidal intent which was not directly expressed or declared but which can be inferred once we look more carefully at the circumstances of the fatal event and of the person concerned. Someone's death in a car crash may, for instance, be the conclusion of an episode in which that person discovers the unfaithfulness of a spouse or lover and then sets out to drive recklessly and aimlessly while in a highly-charged emotional state. In such a case it is extremely difficult to find out what might have been intentional and what accidental in the succession of events. Even when the protagonists in these kinds of episodes survive a crash they are rarely able confidently to elucidate the feelings and intentions they had at the time. When death ensues in such cases a court of law never presumes that suicide has been committed; it returns a verdict of suicide only when intent is provable by evidence such as a letter, written by the person concerned, in which the suicidal intent is explicitly stated. The law's reluctance to return a verdict of suicide is typically exemplified in the recent case of a woman who was found decapitated on a railway line and who had left her dog tied to a fence at the side of the line. She had been chronically and acutely depressed, suffered from tinnitus and agoraphobia, rarely went out alone, and in the five years before her death had seen nineteen different medical consultants. On the morning of the day she died she had been profoundly distressed at the receipt of news of her mother's death. Yet a jury returned an open verdict on her death because there was 'no specific indication she intended to take her life'.

All this shows the law's recognition of two features of intention already referred to in passing when it was pointed out that 'when we know the intention with which someone acts we know both the point of the action and something about the person who acts'. The first feature, spelt out, is that only the person who has an intention can authoritatively say what that intention is. The point is made by Wittgenstein in the *Philosophical Investigations* when he remarks: 'Only you can know if you had that intention'[4]. The second feature is also identified by Wittgenstein:

> Why do I want to tell him about an intention, too, as well as telling him what I did? . . . because I want to tell him something about *myself*, which goes beyond what happened at that time.
>   I reveal to him something of myself when I tell him what I was going to do . . .[5]

These two features of intention form an important background for any discussion of the conceptual and moral issues relating to suicide.

3 WHAT COUNTS AS SUICIDE?

A question that raises a difficulty about the nature of suicide is this: When the intention with which a self-killing is brought about is not so much to render oneself dead but, as in the case of the injured climber, to facilitate some further end by means of one's death, is such a case always to be described as suicide? Perhaps the question could also be put in this way: Does the injured climber, and any person in a comparable situation, *intend* suicide?

Any answer to the first formulation of that question must start, I think, from reflecting on the kind of act that brings about the person's death. If the injured climber deliberately swallows all his pain-relieving tablets in the knowledge that they will poison and kill him, can we possibly say that he has *not* committed suicide? I think it would be difficult to say he has not. But suppose he has rolled himself outside his tent so that it is the cold wind and icy temperature that bring about his death? Is this also suicide? A well-debated example of this kind is the moving and true story of Captain Oates, a member of the group of men who accompanied

Scott on his last expedition to the South Pole. At a time when all the expedition's members were approaching the limits of their endurance and when Oates had become so weak and ill that he felt he might die at any time, he decided he must remove the burden of his presence from his companions. He therefore asked them to leave him in his sleeping bag to die, but they refused. Scott recorded in his diary what then took place:

> He slept through the night before last, hoping not to wake; but he woke in the morning – yesterday. It was blowing a blizzard. He said, 'I am just going outside and may be some time'. He went out into the blizzard and we have not seen him since. . . We knew that poor Oates was walking to his death. . .[6]

In a paper in which he discusses how this death is to be described Professor Roy Holland says that he wants to deny that Oates's death was a suicide. He opposes a view of suicide promulgated by the sociologist, Émile Durkheim, which asserts that all acts of self-renunciation – the martyr dying for faith, the mother sacrificing herself for her child, and comparable acts – are describable as suicide because 'at the moment of acting the victim knows the certain result of his conduct'.[7] Part of Holland's argument rests on the view that Oates's death can scarcely be called a suicide because he does not die by his own hand. He suggests that it is appropriate to say of Oates both that 'he killed himself by going out into the blizzard' and that 'the blizzard killed him', but that there is also a description that is midway between these two: 'He let the blizzard kill him'. Here Holland is using what he calls 'the distinction between doing and suffering' – suffering, that is, in the sense of allowing – to support his claim, although recognizing that it is one that is, in general, fraught with difficulty. He says: 'Had Oates taken out a revolver and shot himself I would have agreed he was a suicide'.[8]

We have to think carefully about Holland's third description of Oates's death: 'He let the blizzard kill him'. It cannot be entirely conceded that Oates did simply allow or suffer the blizzard to kill him; for he went out into the blizzard with the intention of staying in it and of being killed by it. Thus it was not, for example, that, finding himself in difficulty in snow and ice, he simply refrained from shouting for help or trying to extricate himself – certainly a situation describable by the words 'he let the blizzard kill him' – but that he acted positively to put himself where death would inevitably ensue. A further consideration is this: given that one does, in opposition to Durkheim, wish to mark a clear difference between self-sacrificial and other kinds of self-killings, is the distinction Holland uses between suffering and doing actually of much help in marking that difference? For there could be self-killings which, seen in their whole context, one would not want to describe as suicide but in which the person who dies does have, from the nature of the situation, to act positively or even violently in order to die; and it would surely miss the real significance of what Holland is maintaining to think that the description of what such a person did depended more on the means by which death was brought about than on the intention he had in dying. If, for example, the injured climber's only means of ending his life as he lay immobile in his tent was to cut his wrists with his knife which lies to hand at his side, would that fact substantially alter our understanding of what he did and intended?

Perhaps a better way of thinking about the difference between the unequivocal suicide and the self-inflicted death of self-renunciation is to think not so much in terms of a distinction between those who do and those who suffer as between those who take their lives and those who give them. If we think in these terms it is clear that both Oates and the injured climber *gave* their lives with the intention of benefiting their companions. And although the drawing of the distinction between taking and giving by no means establishes an easy rule of the form 'If a life is *given* (by self-killing) then suicide has not been committed', it does indicate, I believe, what is substantially at issue in the reluctance to describe Captain Oates's death as a suicide.

A further way of questioning whether the deaths of Captain Oates and the injured climber were suicides is to apply the second formulation of the question on page 4 to their stories and ask: 'Did they intend suicide?' If we say merely that they did intend suicide this is to misrepresent the significance of what each was aiming to do. But we also have to ask: 'Can it possibly be said of either man that he did *not* intend to commit suicide?' For this, too, looks like some sort of misrepresentation.

A solution that might be offered to this difficulty is to say that each of these men had at least two intentions; that is, each intended both to commit suicide and to achieve a further aim. But that is something which, I think, still sticks in a sensitive craw; not because it is never possible to realize two intentions through the one act – never possible to kill two birds with one stone, so to speak – but because it does not tell us anything at all about the significance and point of what was taking place. For the climber, and for Captain Oates, given the kind of circumstances they were in, there was one thing that was wanted; one bird, if you like, to be aimed at. But in each case the bird needed two stones: the first, death; the second, the change of prospect for others that would then result. Both these men died voluntarily in the sense that they chose to die but, at the same time, it was not death that was wanted but something else. And it is for this reason that their deaths are not suicides. Perhaps, therefore, the most exact account of each man's actions is this: 'He decided to end his life because he intended that his companions should not be impeded by his presence'.

The much-discussed doctrine of double effect does little to help resolve these problems of intention and exoneration. This doctrine is discussed at length in Chapter Seven but, briefly, it distinguishes between what a person intends in his action and the foreseen but unintended results of the action, and it takes a person to intend both the end and the means to the end of his action. If one applies the doctrine to the case of Captain Oates, in order to absolve Oates from charges of suicide one would have to argue that he intended to free his companions from the burden of his presence, that his intended means of doing so was to walk out into the blizzard, and that his death was the foreseen but unintended result of walking out. But this is not convincing. Oates must have intended his death because he would have known that his friends would not have gone on without him unless he was certainly dead. The doctrine of double effect fails to be helpful here because it concentrates on finding morally acceptable descriptions of what it takes to be intentional actions and gives insufficient consideration to what a person's intentions are. It does invoke those distinctions already discussed between letting death occur and positively killing oneself but this does not help to exclude from the category of suicide all those cases we would wish to exclude from it. For, as was pointed out in the discussion of the case of the injured climber, if the person who sacrifices his life is able to do so only by direct and violent means such as cutting his wrists or shooting himself, this does not alter the self-sacrificial intention of his action. To exclude this kind of sacrificial death from the category of suicide we require that other distinction, the one between giving one's life and taking it. This distinction might be marked by referring to the giving as 'ending one's life' and to the taking as 'suicide'.

4 DID SOCRATES COMMIT SUICIDE?

The death of Socrates, as recounted in Plato's dialogue *Phaedo*, raises issues about suicide that are comparable with those already discussed. Socrates' uncompromising moral integrity was a constant source of embarrassment to the political groups which, towards the end of the fifth century BC, were struggling for power in the Athenian state. One of these factions, when it came to power, accused Socrates of not worshipping the gods of the state, of introducing unusual religious practices and of corrupting the young. The penalty for these offences was death but Socrates' accusers probably assumed that he would voluntarily exile himself from Athens and so avoid the charges. He chose instead to stand trial and conduct his own defence. He was found guilty, refused to take up the offer that he should propose his own suitably substantial punishment and was accordingly sentenced to death, the means of death being the self-administered imbibing of a cup of hemlock. During the month that elapsed between sentence and execution he refused to take advantage of an escape arranged for him by his friends, insisting that it would go against his principles and his sense of duty to evade what Athens had decreed. He spent the last day of his life discussing the immortality of the soul with two friend, Cebes and Simmias, and then, voluntarily and before the stipulated hour of sundown, drank the hemlock provided for him. In the conversations that preceded his death Socrates makes it clear that he regards what he is about to do as suicide and that he holds suicide to be wrong 'until God sends some compulsion like the one we are facing now'.[9] He also speaks of a philosopher's attitude to death, saying that it is 'natural that a man who has really devoted his life to philosophy should be cheerful in the face of death, and confident of finding the greatest blessing in the next world';[10] and he says, 'those who really apply themselves in the right way to philosophy are directly and of their own accord preparing themselves for dying and death'.[11] When he asks for the poison to be brought at an earlier hour than is necessary and when Crito tries to restrain him, saying, 'the sun is still upon the mountains . . . no need to hurry', Socrates replies, 'I believe that I should gain nothing by drinking the poison a little later – I should only make myself ridiculous in my own eyes if I clung to life and hugged it when it had no more to offer'.[12]

In a paper called 'Did Socrates Commit Suicide?'[13] R. G. Frey maintains that the conclusion that Socrates did commit suicide is unavoidable. Socrates, he says, did want to die, he intended to drink the hemlock and wanted to drink it either as an end in itself or as a means to some further end and knowing what the consequence would be. He points out that Socrates need not have died by his own hand. He could have refused to drink the hemlock so that his jailer would have had to force him to take it. And he argues that even though Socrates drank the hemlock in the context of a lawful execution commanded by the state, this does not preclude also describing what he did as committing suicide.

Frey considers the claim that Socrates 'does not commit suicide because he does not choose when to die'. He dismisses it by citing cases of self-killing in which the time of death was not chosen but which were, nevertheless, unequivocally cases of suicide. What Frey does not confront is the claim that: 'Socrates does not commit suicide because *he did not choose to commit suicide*'. For although it is true that Socrates drank the hemlock voluntarily in that he chose to drink it himself rather than have it forced into him, and although it is also true that he chose to drink it before the specified time of execution, it is still arguable that what he did is more correctly described as 'acting as a virtuous and honourable Athenian citizen' than as 'committing suicide'. On this view anyone merely declaring that 'Socrates committed suicide' is giving an inadequate description of actions that were the necessary concomitant of what Socrates actually chose and intended to do. This line of thought, opposing Frey's claim that Socrates did commit suicide, can be further developed by considering Socrates' intentions more carefully.

Socrates' declared and overriding intention in all he did was to act virtuously and to be a dutiful citizen, and this included participating in his own execution since the law required that he should administer the hemlock to himself. It may therefore be maintained that although he voluntarily and knowingly brought about his own death, the intention with which he did so was one to which that self-inflicted death was simply the necessary means. Remembering the kind of argument he advanced to suggest that Captain Oates did not commit suicide, we would expect Holland also to defend the view that Socrates did not commit suicide. This he does. He writes:

> Taking hemlock does not, in the context of an Athenian judicial execution, amount to slaughtering onself: in this circumstance it is no more an act of suicide than the condemned man's walk to the scaffold in our society.[14]

I want very much to go along with the distinctions Holland is making. They seem to me to pick out exactly the reasons why we may hesitate to describe deaths such as those of Captain Oates and Socrates as suicides. But Holland's analogy between Socrates' taking of the hemlock and the modern condemned man's walk to the scaffold does not seem to be correct. For the drinking of the hemlock actually brought about the process of Socrates' dying, and Socrates administered the hemlock to himself. But the condemned man's walk to the scaffold does not bring about his dying, for when he has completed his walk to the scaffold he has not begun to die. A correct analogy with Socrates' drinking of the hemlock is therefore with a condemned man who actually presses the switch to operate the device that kills him, so that he is his own executioner. This changed analogy would provide us with the remark that Socrates' taking of the hemlock '. . . is no more an act of suicide than the condemned man's act of pressing the switch that activates the electric chair'. Surprisingly, perhaps, making the analogy more exact in this way actually does no harm to the point Holland is making. For the point would only be harmed if it were now unequivocally clear that we would call the death of the man who pressed the switch for his own execution a suicide, so that, by analogy, Socrates' death is also describable as suicide. But it is most unlikely that this kind of death would be described as suicide when the accurate and explicit description 'self-execution' is available for it. If, within a judicial system, criminals sentenced to death were given the choice either of pressing the switch for themselves or of having it pressed by an executioner, we would not see in a newspaper reporting such a case a headline that declared: 'Condemned man commits suicide', for then we would suppose that the man had killed himself in some way in his cell while awaiting the day of execution. An appropriate headline would be something such as: 'Condemned man opts for self-execution'. Holland's claim that 'taking hemlock does not, in the context of an Athenian judicial execution, amount to slaughtering oneself' remains unimpaired even when his analogy is sharpened.

One thing that became clear in the discussion of intention was that we know something about a person's intention when we know what he or she wants. Knowing, for instance, that the injured climber wants above all that the climbing team will succeed in its venture helps us to comprehend what he intends by his death. That connection between wanting and intending can be invoked by someone wishing to argue that Socrates *did* commit suicide. For, it may be pointed out, not only did Socrates drink the hemlock in full knowledge of what the consequence would be, but he also seems to have wanted death since, in the days before his execution, he talks of the life of a philosopher as being a preparation for death and follows that discussion with a remark about not wishing to cling to life 'when it had no more to offer'. This looks like a forceful point. However, I think we have to ask whether Socrates would have been entertaining the idea of ending his life had it not been for his trial and the sentence passed upon him. Since he explicitly states that he held suicide to be wrong 'until God sends some compulsion like the one we are facing now' we cannot suppose that, in the absence of that compulsion, he would have been planning to end his life. Nor does his preparedness for death suggest a preparedness to kill himself in order to arrive at it. Plato's account in the *Phaedo* nowhere suggests that here was a man wishing to die and seizing the opportunity of his trial to arrange that he did so in a dramatic and moving way. Holland puts this matter very succinctly. He says: 'Socrates had a wish for death and thought it his business as a philosopher to "practise dying" but not to practise suicide, which he said should be committed by no one'.[15]

5   KNOWLEDGE OF INTENTIONS

Let us look at a case that is very different from that of Socrates or Captain Oates but which produces kindred difficulties once the description 'suicide' is given to it. Suppose my death is being prematurely and rapidly brought about because I am addicted to alcohol. Someone, seeing the way I am going, may say to me by way of reproach, 'You are committing suicide'. But am I? I may reply that even though I know that I will soon die as the result of my drinking I none the less am not committing suicide because in drinking to excess I do not intend to kill myself any more than I intend having a hangover in the morning; and although it will probably be correct to say of me 'She drank herself to death', it will not be so to say that 'She committed suicide'. The accusative 'You are committing suicide' accordingly has to be understood as a kind of metaphor that is used in an attempt to make my plight vivid to me. Death, I am being told, will be the result, even if it is not the aim, of my drinking; and since I know and am already experiencing the harm my addiction does to me it is *as if* I intend my death in the way the suicide proper does.

A psychological view may be invoked to support the judgement that I am committing suicide. It might be suggested that I have a covert and long-term desire to kill myself and that this is being expressed through my addiction to alcohol. Others, I may be told, may manifest a similar wish by indulging in heavy smoking, over-eating or under-eating, anti-social behaviour, dangerous pursuits or through accident-proneness. But there are difficulties with this view. First there is the difficulty of distinguishing between, on the one hand, instances of what might be called straightforward addictions, constitutional clumsiness that generates mishaps and likings for adventurous activities and, on the other hand, death wishes disguised in those forms. And in the latter cases, when the disguised or covert desire to end one's life is posited as an unconscious one, a further difficulty arises; for the suggestion now seems to be that I might well have the intention to destroy myself but not know that I have it although it seems likely to others that I do have it. Yet, on the understanding so far gleaned of intention, it is the agent who is deemed to be the final authority on what his or her intention is. Can one then be said to have an intention that may be known to others but not to oneself?

It is not necessary, here and now, to explore the concept of intention in its fullest detail. But we do need to dispel any confusion that relates to the present issue about whether the person who destroys herself through an addiction can properly be described as a suicide in the face of her denial of an intention to commit suicide. We have first to recognize that when intention is characterized by saying, as Wittgenstein says, 'Only you can know if you had that intention', this is not the same as saying 'You always do know if you had that intention'. Wittgenstein's remark brings out the point that intention is an important aspect of one's self, and that if anyone *can* know what one's intention is then that person is oneself. But it does not follow that each person's intentions are always known to herself or himself. It is therefore entirely feasible that I could be unaware that in drinking to excess I am manifesting an intention to destroy myself. It is also possible, and typical in numerous psychotherapeutic case histories, that I might come to see as the outcome of psychotherapy that I am indeed manifesting an intention, not previously recognized, to kill myself. However, just as the law will not record a verdict of suicide unless there is clear evidence of a declared suicidal intention on the part of the person concerned, so is there a similar reluctance – one might call it a conceptual reluctance – to ascribe suicidal intention to any person who sincerely and consistently denies such an intention, however coherent a picture of someone hell-bent on self-destruction is being presented to the therapist or observer. In a discussion of a Freudian understanding of this kind of situation, A. C. MacIntyre has argued that two elements must be taken into account when considering intention and that both elements are essential in both the ordinary and Freudian concepts of intention. He calls one of these elements 'the pattern in the behaviour' and the other 'the possibility of avowal'. He writes:

> Freud argues that certain types of neurotic behaviour are the result of unconscious motivation. The neurotic has purposes and intentions of which he is unaware. Since he is unaware of them he cannot avow them. Freud would seem to be using 'intention' here to refer to a pattern of behaviour. But an essential feature of psychoanalysis is the way in which the neurotic comes to recognise and to acknowledge the purpose of his acts. It is only when this has come about that he is able to redirect his intentions, to alter his behaviour in the light of his new self-knowledge. This acknowledgement by the patient confirms the analyst's interpretation of the motivation of the neurotic behaviour. And unless the patient will *in the end* avow his intention the analyst's interpretation of his behaviour is held to be mistaken.[16]

MacIntyre's analysis of intention is helpful. It enables us to see more clearly the features of intention we have been exploring in the cases so far considered. It also extends our understanding of the concept in giving weight to something that Wittgenstein's remarks do not cover, namely, that a person's intention is something about which we are entitled to hypothesize and that any such hypothesis is based on observation of behaviour. But he affirms also that a person's intention is not established unless the hypothesis is endorsed by means of the 'avowal' of the person whose intention is thus conjectured about. It is just these two features of behaviour and avowal that have been invoked in one way or another in the discussions of the deaths we have been considering so far.

6 'REVENGE' SUICIDE

The statistics of the social sciences inform us that a large number of suicides are 'revenge suicides'; that is, are suicides committed with the intention of punishing or hurting another person. Suppose the case of a husband who has been deserted by his wife for someone else with whom she now lives happily, and who kills himself in some shocking way in order to destroy the woman's happiness by making her feel guilt for his death and shame and regret for what she has done. This case is formally similar to the cases of Captain Oates and the injured climber in that it is one of a self-inflicted death that is instrumental in achieving an aim that is other than and further to the death. For it is not that the husband, angry, bitter and wretched though he is, wishes so much to end his life as that he sees a shocking suicidal death as being the perfect weapon for the wound he wishes to inflict. We therefore have to ask if it should now be argued, as it was in the cases of Captain Oates and the injured climber, that this man's self-killing is not to be described as suicide on the grounds that his intention, like the intentions of the other two, was not so much to end his life as to achieve some further aim.

Certainly one would want to point out, as with Captain Oates, the climber, and Socrates as well, that there is more to this man's story than a direct resolve to end his life: one would want to explain that 'he acted to procure revenge' just as one would want to explain that Oates 'acted out of a profound concern for his friends'. But having said that, there seems to be little reason for withholding the description 'suicide' from this death. And this is surely because its agent falls without equivocation into the category of those who take their lives rather than into that of those who, like Captain Oates, the injured climber and Socrates, give them.

7   THE MORAL ISSUES

What does the foregoing discussion show us about our understanding of the nature of·suicide? It brings out very clearly something we have known all along and that has underlain the points of view and arguments we have examined; namely, that there is a widely held and deeply felt opinion that there is something profoundly reprehensible about suicide. Why else should anyone strive either to exclude noble and self-sacrificial self-killings from its category or to spell out the special circumstances that justify and ennoble them? What has also become apparent is that because suicide is something done by the self to the self, any view of the morality of suicide will be related to some considered view of the human self. It will reflect judgements about the status of the self, its degree of autonomy and self-dominion, its relationship to other selves and to God. Because it is something done by the self to the self, suicide is essentially a personal moral matter; and because it is an act that ends a life, reflection on it generates questions about the meaning of life. Consideration of the morality of suicide is therefore inadequate if it is confined to an examination of the immediate issues of everyday living. For here is an act that is not so much a part of life as a judgement on it and that is more an expression or declaration of character and attitude than the working out of some purpose within the world. Any moral theory that purports to provide a framework for thinking about issues to do with suicide must accordingly be able to treat a very broad range of matters. It must be able to engage with questions about whether suicide is always and in itself wrong, whether any such wrongness may be mitigated under certain conditions, or whether it is an act that receives its moral colouring from the circumstances, characters and purposes of those committing it. It must also be sensitive to the kinds of metaphysical, personal and religious issues that are so readily generated by reflection on suicide.

8 SUICIDE AND THE LAW

Although there are certain communities, movements and cultures in which suicide is not only acceptable but honourable, aversion to it is widespread and seems to run very deep. In the past, legislation has done much to endorse and maintain this natural aversion to self-killing. In Britain, until the mid-twentieth century, suicide was regarded by the law as a crime that ranked with homicide or murder. Homicide is the act by one human being of killing another human being. An act of homicide is said to be *justifiable* if it is unavoidably necessary, if it is done in order to prevent a dreadful crime, or if it is carried out in obedience to the law. It is *excusable* when committed in self-defence or by misadventure; it is *felonious* when it is the wilful killing of a person through malice aforethought and in these latter cases it is murder. An unlawful killing carried out in a sudden passion or involuntarily in the course of committing an unlawful action is not a felony but manslaughter. A felony is a crime of a much graver nature than any of those generally classified as 'misdemeanours' and, during the time that it was an unlawful act, suicide could properly be described as a *felo de se*, or self-murder, since it was committed intentionally or with malice aforethought. A passage from William Blackstone's *Commentaries on the Laws of England*, published in 1769, amply exhibits the seriousness of a felony and at the same time shows plainly the cast of opinion concerning suicide that prevailed at the time and that changed only very slowly in the succeeding two hundred years:

> . . . the law of England wisely and religiously considers that no man hath a power to destroy life but by commission from God, the author of it: and, as the suicide is guilty of a

double offence; one spiritual, in invading the prerogative of the Almighty and rushing into his immediate presence uncalled for; the other temporal, against the king, who hath an interest in the preservation of all his subjects; the law hath therefore ranked this among the highest crimes, making it a peculiar species of felony, a felony committed on one's self.[17]

Blackstone goes on to say that anyone who counsels another to kill himself is guilty of murder if the counsel is followed. He also points out that 'the party must be of years of discretion and in his senses, else it is no crime'. He urges coroners' juries not to acquit every suicide on the assumption that the very act of suicide is evidence of insanity, because 'the law very rationally judges that every melancholy or hypochondriac fit does not deprive a man of the capacity of discerning right from wrong'. A lunatic who kills himself in a lucid interval, he says, is a *felo de se* as much as any other person. The thought that suicide is at once unnatural, irreligious and socially disgraceful is reflected in the kind of punishment Blackstone advocates for it. He asks: 'What punishment can human laws inflict on one who has withdrawn himself from their reach?' And he answers:

> They can only act upon what he has left behind him, his reputation and fortune; on the former by an ignominious burial in the highway, with a stake driven through his body; on the latter by a forfeiture of all his goods and chattels to the king; hoping that his care for either his own reputation or the welfare of his family would be some motive to restrain him from so desperate and wicked an act.[18]

9 THE HISTORICAL DIMENSION

In spite of the religious, moral and social condemnations of suicide embodied in Blackstone's *Commentaries* there does not seem to have been any time in recorded history when suicide was not practised and was not defended, at any rate by some, as well as condemned. Its morality has therefore been debated at length and in considerable detail. Those who disapprove of suicide have seen in it a double terribleness. The first terribleness is that of a life's being ended before it has fully run its natural course; the second, which compounds the first and which has made suicide, for many, the most sinful and criminal of all acts, is the terribleness of wilfully inflicting death upon oneself. Those who do not disapprove of suicide have seen nothing necessarily wrong either with the idea that one might choose to die before one's life came to a natural end or with the idea that one's death might then be self-inflicted. It is illuminating to look at some of the historical aspects of this debate; for then it is possible to see how the inadequacies of one kind of approach are dealt with by a succeeding or alternative view and how one emphasis gives way to another. How, for example, the centre of gravity for moral reflection has changed by shifting between the ideas of divine authority, societal well-being and the sovereignty of the individual. The tensions between these three are particularly acute in a consideration of suicide. Perhaps an even more important benefit of looking at the debate about suicide in an historical context is that, in spite of some profound changes that have taken place in the way in which human beings think of themselves, it enables one to focus on the persisting and recurring issues that suicide generates and to discern what it essentially requires from a moral theory. That historical context is the setting for the next chapter.

NOTES

1 For a discussion of Dadaism and suicide, see Alvarez, A. (1971) *The Savage God*, Weidenfeld and Nicolson, Chapter 6.
2 *Seppuku/Hara-Kiri*: This was, until 1873, a method of punishment that allowed offenders of rank to execute themselves. It dates from the twelfth century. 'It was not mere suicide. It was an institution, legal and ceremonial . . . by which warriors could expiate their friends or prove their sincerity' (Harada, T. (1914) *Faith of Japan*, New York, p. 129). Hara-kiri was usually performed in a three-sided enclosure hung with white curtains. The condemned man, wearing special clothing, sat on a blue mattress and was attended by a friend. With a short sword he made a horizontal and then a vertical cut in his abdomen. It was then the duty of his attendant friend to behead him.

Seppuku and other forms of suicide practised in Japan are described in Farberow, Norman L. (1975) *Suicide in Different Cultures*, University Park Press, Chapter 17.

3 Stevie Smith (1975) *Collected Poems*, Penguin.

4 Wittgenstein, L. (1968) *Philosophical Investigations*, G. E. M. Anscombe (trans.), Blackwell, Section 247.

5 *Ibid.*, Section 659.

6 Scott, R. F. (1935) *Scott's Last Expedition*, John Murray, vol. I, p. 462.

7 Holland, R. F., 'Suicide', in Vesey, G. (ed.) (1969) *Talk of God*, Macmillan, p. 73.

8 *Ibid.*, p. 80.

9 Plato, 'Phaedo', in Tredennick, Hugh (trans.) (1959) *The Last Days of Socrates*, Penguin, p. 105, 61c–62d.

10 *Ibid.*, p. 107.

11 *Ibid.*

12 *Ibid.*, p. 181.

13 Frey, R. G. (1978) 'Did Socrates Commit Suicide?', *Philosophy*, 53.

14 Holland, *op. cit.*, p. 75.

15 *Ibid.*, p. 74.

16 MacIntyre, A. C. (1958) *The Unconscious*, Routledge & Kegan Paul, p. 560.

17 Blackstone, William, (1836) *Commentaries on the Laws of England*, vol. IV.

18 *Ibid.*

CHAPTER TWO

The historical debate on suicide

1 SUICIDE DEFENDED

A major landmark in the debate about suicide is a defence of it written by John Donne (1573–1631), the metaphysical poet who became Dean of St Paul's. Donne's defence is called *Biathanatos*.[1] The word is a contracted form of *biaio thanatos*, a Greek term meaning 'dying a violent death' and used most frequently of suicides. 'Suicide' was not in use until the 1650s, almost half a century after *Biathanatos* was written and Donne, in the main, uses the term 'self-homicide'. A term that was in currency early in the seventeenth century and that reflects the prevailing though by no means unchallenged attitude of the time is 'self-murder'. In 1608, the year in which Donne wrote *Biathanatos*, William Vaughan asked 'Whether selfe-murther be lawfull for the cause of God's glory?'[2]

Donne's approach is made plain in the lengthy subtitle to *Biathanatos*: 'A Declaration of that Paradox or Thesis, that Self-homicide is not so naturally Sin that it may never be otherwise. Wherein the Nature, and the extent of all those Laws which seem to be violated by this Act are diligently surveyed.' It is clear from this that Donne is going to argue that suicide is not intrinsically wrong or evil and that some suicides may therefore be sinless. The 'paradox' of the position he advances seems to be that an act which may sometimes be seen as a sin may not always be seen so.

In what general setting was Donne putting forward his

position? He had to oppose formidable views: the well-considered and well-entrenched pronouncements of religion, society and the law, grounded in a reverence for life, strengthened by social expediency and firmly supported by the exertion of power and authority. These views were a rich amalgam of pre-Christian and Christian ideas. In ancient Greece, suicide had been largely tolerated and was approved and recommended by Cynic, Stoic and Epicurean philosophers. But according to Plato Socrates did not approve of suicide, although Plato himself makes exception for those who killed themselves in intolerable circumstances of distress or disgrace. Aristotle condemned suicide as cowardly, even though he admitted that 'the suicide braves death',[3] and maintained that it was also an injustice against the state because 'the man who cuts his throat in a fit of temper is voluntarily doing an injury which the law does not allow'.[4] The Greek burial custom of severing the hand of a suicide and burying it apart from the body suggests that there must have been general unease at the thought of a self-inflicted death.

In ancient Rome eminent Romans, including Cato and Seneca, chose to kill themselves and were thought noble for doing so. Immanual Kant (1724–1804) gives a lucid account of Cato's story:

> Cato knew that the entire Roman nation relied upon him in their resistance to Caesar, but he found that he could not prevent himself from falling into Caesar's hands. What was he to do? If he, the champion of freedom, submitted, everyone would say, 'If Cato himself submits, what else can we do?' If, on the other hand, he killed himself, his death might spur on the Romans to fight to the bitter end in defence of their freedom. So he killed himself. He thought that it was necessary for him to die. He thought that if he could not go on living as Cato, he could not go on living at all. It must certainly be admitted that in a case such as this, where suicide is a virtue, appearances are in its favour.[5]

The general opinion of Roman aristocrats was that 'he is at liberty to die who does not wish to live'. But at the same time a clear distinction was observed between honourable and dishonourable suicide. A cowardly self-killing was seen as particularly ignominious. Roman felons, slaves and soldiers were punished for any unsuccessful attempts at suicides that were motivated by the desire to escape their duties rather than by special circumstances of pain and distress. And Cato's thoughts about whether he should or should not kill himself were directed almost entirely towards ensuring that his death would be seen as an unequivocally courageous example to his followers.

The curious mix of natural and religious sentiment, superstition, ambivalence, and reasoned argument that characterized Greek and Roman thinking about suicide was inherited by early Christianity. Little guidance for Christians could be derived from the Old Testament which contains six instances of suicide, none of which is unequivocally condemned and two of which are praised. In the New Testament there is one suicide, that of Judas Iscariot who hanged himself after betraying Jesus, and one attempted suicide, that of Paul's jailer, who tried to kill himself for fear of the punishment he would receive when his prisoners escaped. The first clear statement of Christian doctrine on suicide was formulated by St Augustine (354–430) who condemned it on the grounds that it violated the sixth commandment, 'Thou shalt not kill', that it denied the opportunity for repentance and that it was a cowardly act. In 533 the second Council of Orleans denied funeral rites to suicides who were also criminals. In 563 the Council of Barga forbade the Christian burial of suicides and in 590 the Council of Antisidor forbade the Church to accept offerings for the souls of suicides. In the thirteenth century Thomas Aquinas endorsed Augustine's views and declared against suicide on three counts. He maintained that it was altogether unlawful to kill oneself, first, because it is contrary to natural law; second, because to do so injures the community by depriving it of one of its members; third, because life is God's gift to man and 'it belongs to God alone to pronounce sentence of death and life. . .' Meanwhile civil law had absorbed Roman sanctions against suicides. The goods and sometimes the lands of convicted *felos de se*, that is, persons who had committed violent crimes against themselves, were taken by the crown and their bodies were buried at crossroads with stakes driven through their chests.

The Christian Church's attitude to suicide as articulated by Augustine and Aquinas was developed into a powerful and influential doctrine. But it was not accepted without question. The humanism and individualism that developed from and within the revival of classical learning in the fifteenth and sixteenth centuries produced an intellectual temperament that was both inquiring and critical and that compared what it learnt about the attitudes of Greece and Rome with contemporary attitudes. The debate on suicide was therefore fully alive and its arguments were well rehearsed in many European minds when Donne took up his pen to write *Biathanatos*. His credentials were entirely appropriate to his task. He had absorbed the Aristotelianism disseminated by the teaching of St Thomas Aquinas and the medieval schoolmen and he had spent several years studying both civil and canon law. He was equally conversant with all kinds of theological controversy and was a restless questioner of all points of religious doctrine, one who, self-confessedly, could come to no resolution 'till I had, to the measure of my poor wit and judgement, surveyed and digested the whole body of Divinity, controverted between ours and the Roman Church'.[6] His temperament, too, was aptly suited to his task. He was disposed to dwell, at times with a wistful longing, on the act of self-annihilation. Relating the story of the attempted suicide of a man called Beza who, 'only for the anguish of a scurf, which over ran his head, . . . had once drowned himself from the Millers bridge in *Paris* if his *Uncle*, by chance had not then come that way', Donne admits, 'I have often such a sickly inclination'.[7] But this propensity in Donne did not mean that his defence of suicide was a merely idiosyncratic outburst. Perplexity and interest concerning the morality of suicide was widespread. S. E. Sprott, in his study of the development of the suicide controversy in the seventeenth and eighteenth centuries, calls *Biathanatos* 'a tract for the times that treated a subject of emerging public, not perversely personal interest'.[8]

2 BIATHANATOS

Donne's subtitle to his tract, as we have seen, has declared
that he will diligently survey all the laws which seem to be
violated by the act of self-homicide and we understand from
this that he is going to show that self-homicide only *seems*
to violate those laws or that it does not always violate them.
He finds three reasons why suicide was generally condemned.
First, because it was assumed to proceed from desperation;
second, because of a belief, adhered to by some, in the
impossibility of penitence; third, because since it was presumed to be a sin and so unpardonable without repentance,
suicide was thought to be unpardonable because the act itself
makes repentance impossible.

Despair was held to be sinful because it showed infidelity
in the face of the Christian command to hope. Donne
endeavours to weaken this stance. He points out that not all
despair is sinful, and cites examples of what he takes to be
sinless despair. It is not sinful, he says, 'in a Priest employed
to convert Infidels . . . to despair that God would give him
the power of Miracles'.[9] More to the point, he argues that
many suicides are committed without despair: 'many . . .
have proceeded therein as religiously as in a Sacrifice'.[10] This
is an important point in a defence of suicide and should not be
dismissed as one that had greater sharpness in a seventeenth-
century context than it has now. If one thinks of typical
modern cases of suicide one quickly recognizes not only that
nearly all of them are, in one way or another, the outcome
of feelings of despair but also that this yielding to despair,
the suicide's giving up or giving in, is still what makes the
act, for many, a reprehensible and shameful one. Part of the
case made by Roy Holland when he wishes to maintain that
Captain Oates's death should not be counted as a suicide is
to point out that Oates did not act out of despair, that there
was nothing reprehensible in what he did and that for these
reasons what he did should not go under the name of suicide.
He says of Oates that

> He had borne intense suffering for weeks without complaint
> . . . but remained cheerful right to the end. The sentiment
> that he was entitled to quit or that anyway he was going to

quit, never entered into it. Accordingly I want to deny he was a suicide. . .[11]

Donne's response to the second condemnation of suicide, that is, to the view that some people are pre-ordained not to be capable of penitence, is to maintain that we are no more justified in specifying some people as incapable of penitence than we are in specifying some others as sinless. This leaves as the only basis of the view that suicide makes repentance impossible the claim that the act itself, by ending life, precludes repentance. Donne then argues that since there is no certainty that self-homicide is sinful we should lean towards making the most charitable judgement possible of it, since this is what the Church, 'so indulgent and liberal to her children',[12] always does. His examples of this liberality are copious and he deploys them ingeniously. He ends his introductory analysis by citing Aquinas's definition of sin as the contravention of the laws of Nature, Reason and God. This gives what follows in his tract a three-part structure, for he is going to consider each kind of law in turn and to maintain that none of them is always contravened by suicide.

3 SUICIDE NOT AGAINST NATURE

Donne's way of proceeding is to invoke everything he can think of to show that suicide might not always be sinful. Sometimes he simply cites what others have done or said in order to add authority or precedent to his own view, and many of his arguments are redolent of the scholastic casuistry and rhetoric in which he was well-practised. Against the view that self-homicide contravenes the Law of Nature he first points out that the term 'Law of Nature' is used so variously that it is difficult to know exactly what is to be understood by it. But he can, he says, find no meaning of it that justifies a claim that self-homicide contravenes it. Many things that we tend to regard as sin or evil were done by Abraham and the Israelites at the command of God and this shows, Donne argues, that evil is not part of the nature of the thing or deed, nor is it 'in the Nature of the whole harmony of the world, and therefore in no Law of Nature'[13] but consists rather in the violating of a commandment. The main charge he has to consider here is that suicide is against nature in that it violates the natural law that commands self-preservation. He meets this charge by declaring that all the precepts of natural law are contained in the abjuration to 'Fly Evil, seeke Good',[14] and that in the case of human beings this means that we must 'Do according to Reason', reason being natural to human beings. Self-preservation, he continues, is certainly part of the Law of Nature; but so is Liberty, and just as I may reason that in order to save my life if taken prisoner I should give up my liberty and become a slave, so may I, under the same circumstances, reason that self-homicide would be the greater good; and neither of these courses of action is against the general Law of Nature that commends a person to 'Fly Evil, seeke Good'.

Donne has other reasons for not thinking suicide a contravention of the Law of Nature. One is that 'in all Ages, in all places, upon all occasions, men of all conditions have affected it, and inclined to do it'.[15] He cites numerous examples, some of them bizarre, of such self-killings:

> *Aristarchus*, when he saw that 72 years, nor the corrupt and malignant disease of being a severe Critique could wear him out, starved himself . . . *Homer*, who had written a thousand things, which no man else understood, is said to have hanged himself because he understood not the fisherman's riddle . . . *Portia*, *Cato's* daughter . . . died by swallowing burning coals . . . Poor *Terence*, because he lost his 108, translated Comedies, drowned himself . . . And *Zeno*, before whom scarce any is preferred, because he stumbled and hurt his finger against the ground, interpreted that as a summons from the earth and hanged himself, being then almost 100 years old.[16]

He refers, too, to various phenomena of mass suicides deriving either from custom or hysteria: the *Soldieros* of Caesar's time in France who, 'enjoying many benefits and commodities from men of higher rank, always when the Lord died celebrated his funeral with their own'; the same practice 'in all the Wives of the kingdom of *Bengala* in the *Indies*'; 'those swarms of the *Roman* Gladiatory Champions, which . . . in some one Month cost *Europe* 30,000 Men, and to which exercise and profession of Life, till express laws forbad it, not only men of great birth and place in the state, but also women coveted to be admitted'.[17] He reminds his readers in detail and at length how diligently martyrdom had been sought by thousands and how glorious their deaths were thought to be. His last observation against the view that suicide contravenes the Law of Nature that enjoins self-preservation is that the legal systems of many states either deployed self-killing, as in Socrates' Athens, so that 'condemned men were their own Executioners by poison',[18] or advocated it under certain conditions. Sir Thomas More, he tells us, 'a man of the most tender and delicate Conscience that the world saw since Aug: [Augustine]', had the priests and magistrates in his ideal state, Utopia, 'exhort Men affected with Miserable diseases to kill themselves'.[19]

4 SUICIDE NOT AGAINST REASON

When Donne turns to considering the claim that self-homicide is against Reason he brings the whole weight of his legal knowledge to bear on the matter, for he regards civil and canon law as: 'Conclusions, drawn and deduced from the primary Reason by our discourse, and Ratiocination'.[20] He finds that civil law, with only two exceptions, 'hath pronounced nothing against this self-homicide'.[21] The first exception is the edict of the Emperor Adrian in AD 120 which condemned those Roman soldiers, already mentioned on p. 23, who attempted suicide in order to avoid dangerous duties, but which forbade punishment if the reasons were those of misery and grief. The second exception is the law which required that the goods of an accused man be confiscated if he commits suicide before judgement is pronounced. Canon or ecclesiastical law, Donne reminds us, is greater in its scope than civil law in that it governs rulers as well as peoples, and it is greater in its object since it is concerned with eternal rather than earthly matters. It is also, he says, 'apt to presume, or believe a guiltiness upon light Evidence, because those punishments ever work good effects, whether just or no'.[22] Thus if he can show that canon law, with its aptitude to presume guilt, is not against self-homicide, he will be strengthening his case considerably.

Donne says that he can find nothing in canon law that names self-homicide as a heresy or a sin, or that punishes it. However, he cannot ignore the decrees of the Councils of 553, 563 and 590, listed on p. 23, which forbade the practice of some Christian funeral rites in certain cases of suicide. He therefore engages all his skill in casuistry and his comprehensive knowledge of historical and legal facts in arguing at length that these edicts show up as far less severe, or even trivial, once placed in their full and correct contexts, and he claims that in the case of the Council of Antisidor's decree that forbade the Church to accept offerings for the soul of suicides 'neither was it much obligatory, or considerable . . . being only a diocesan council of one Bishop and his Abbots'.[23] In contrast with this extended treatment of canon law he deals very briskly with the particular law of state which decreed that he who kills himself without just cause is a *felo de se* and must forfeit his goods, they then being put to charitable use. This *felo de se*, Donne admits, was regarded as murder, yet, he continues 'the reasons alleged there, are but these, that the King hath lost a Subject, that his peace is broken, and that it is of evil Example'.[24]

Donne's light dismissal of those last three points against suicide suggests that it was much less important for him to meet charges that suicide was socially or politically harmful, disruptive or shocking, than to meet those that declared it to be against divine law. Morality for him, and for his time, was essentially dependent on religion rather than on societal interests or the individual conscience. Of course, this is not to say that society and the individual carried no weight in considerations of morality, but that what weight they had was subservient to the primary concern with divine authority. At the end of his review of the civil laws and customs that were against suicide Donne has found that 'none of those laws which prescribe civil restraints from doing it can make it sin'.[25]

What becomes clear as one reads *Biathanatos* is that Donne at no point wishes to absolve every suicide from blame. He agrees, he says, with St Augustine that suicide is not justified

if it is committed in order to evade difficulties, to punish
ourselves, to prevent others or ourselves from sinning, or
to advance into the next life except when that advance is
primarily for the glory of God. But he opposes Thomas
Aquinas's prohibitions on suicide. Against Aquinas's objection that suicide is harmful in that it deprives the state of a
member, he argues that this might be said of any person
who ceases to serve the state, 'whether in this Life or the
next'.[26] Aquinas's position here is rather weak in that his
declared view can be used to argue that there are certain
circumstances under which a person ought to commit, rather
than refrain from, suicide. For if a reason for not committing
suicide is that it does harm to the state then it is possible to
argue that suicide could be permissible and even desirable
as a means of preventing such harm. But Donne's reply is
also weak. For all it shows is that suicide is not the only
way in which the state may be deprived of a member, and
it does not follow from that that suicide is not wrong.

5   SUICIDE NOT AGAINST GOD

When Donne considers, in the third part of *Biathanatos*,
whether self-homicide is against the law of God, he systematically goes through the Bible to see what condemnations
of the act it contains. He finds nothing in all the Law of
Moses that is against suicide. But the sixth commandment,
'Thou shalt not kill', presents a formidable difficulty for
him, for Augustine had decided that this applied as much
to killing oneself as to killing another person. Donne says,
'I must have leave to depart from St Aug: opinion here',[27]
and his main argument against Augustine's view is that there
are cases in which to kill oneself is permissible because it
serves a higher law. He cites a complicated example, that of
a 'public exemplary Person' whose life sets a pattern for
many and who is 'forced by a Tyrant' to perform an act of
idolatry. Although the exemplary person can satisfy his
private conscience that he has not sinned in performing the
act of idolatry, the public interpretation of the act is otherwise
and cannot be corrected. In such a case, Donne says,

'perchance he were better kill himself'.[28] He argues that this kind of self-homicide is justified because it puts God's glory 'above all human respects'.

Donne finds several biblical references that suggest to him that there is no unqualified divine injunction against self-killing. From a consideration of St Paul's words, 'Though I give my body to be burned, and have no love, it profiteth no thing', he concludes that such a death was highly esteemed and so not against the Law of Nature. In Christ's remark that 'the good shepherd gives his life for his sheep' he finds a further justification for ending one's own life. He reminds us, too, that Christ said, 'The greatest Love is to bestow his Life for his friends. In which and all of this kind, we must remember, that we are commanded to do it so, as *Christ* did it'.[29] Once again, the point being made is that the act of self-homicide is not sinful if it is done for the right reason. It is noteworthy that all the biblical passages invoked by Donne are about the sacrificing of life for the sake of some noble or altruistic purpose. There is no suggestion here from him that the pre-Christian sentiment that 'he is at liberty to die who does not wish to live' would be supported by the Bible.

6   A JUDGEMENT ON LIFE

In this brief survey of Donne's defence of suicide I have had to select particular aspects of it for consideration and to ignore or gloss over many of his subtle and casuistic arguments. But what I hope the survey has shown is that in spite of an important difference between centres of cultural gravity in the early seventeenth century and the late twentieth century – roughly speaking, between a predominantly religious centre of gravity then and a predominantly secular one now – many of the questions about suicide that exercised Donne are fundamentally similar to those that exercise us now. Although there is not now such a widespread and straightforward acceptance of the notion that one's life is a gift from God for which gratitude should be shown, there is nevertheless a general respect for life that, even in its most secular form, derives from a view of ourselves that has remained largely unchanged in the shift from a religious to a secular orientation. One part of this view that is common to both the religious and the secular standpoints is the belief that human beings tend, under most circumstances, to manifest a natural instinct to self-preservation. Another part of it is the belief that whatever originating source our lives and the world may have, it is certainly not we, except in a narrowly biological and temporal sense, who are that originating source. A third part of this enduring view of ourselves consists of our prevailing awareness of the transience of earthly life. And although it might at first be thought that our present, twentieth-century sense of human transience must differ radically from any such sense in the seventeenth century, when a transient and earthly life was seen by many as a preliminary to an eternal and heavenly one rather than as the only life one might have, this difference is not something which, in the end, seems substantially to affect the part that awareness of transience plays in our reflections on suicide. This is not to suggest that secular and religious persons will come to similar conclusions about the morality or otherwise of suicide, but that, in reflecting on the matter, both will be much concerned with questions relating to the three things I have mentioned; namely, human nature, the question of the source of all things, and the transience of earthly life. Perhaps it is because of concern with these aspects of human existence that, in the development of Western views, suicide has come to be thought of as something that is not so much within or part of a life as an expression of a judgement on it, and a manifestation of the individuality and the values of the person concerned.

7   DAVID HUME ON SUICIDE

Biathanatos was not published until 1646, almost forty years after it was written and fifteen years after Donne's death. Its second edition appeared in 1700 and encountered a much-changed climate of opinion. England had experienced civil war, regicide, protectorate rule and the restoration of the monarchy, and one outcome of all this and of the general intellectual upheaval in seventeenth-century England was a much stronger affirmation of the use of reason and of the significance of individual thought. The years from 1683 to 1720 have been described as 'the libertine era of suicide' and as the incidence of suicide increased so did the arguments for and against it. In the 1750s the Scottish philosopher, David Hume, wrote an essay, 'Of Suicide'.[30] Its tone and approach exhibit the changes that had been taking place: the movement from a God-oriented morality to a socially-oriented one, and the increase in reliance on the use of reason.

Hume broaches his subject by pointing out that philosophy is the supreme antidote 'to superstition and false religion', succeeding where other remedies fail. The superstitious man, made miserable by his thraldom, hesitates, he says, even to kill himself in order to end his misery because he fears to offend his maker. Because we are superstitious we fear to use our freedom to take the step that would 'remove us from the regions of pain and sorrow'; and the 'menaces' of superstition, he declares, 'chain us down to a hated being, which she herself chiefly contributes to render miserable'.[31]

Hume's aim is 'to restore men to their native liberty by examining all the common arguments against suicide, and shewing that that action may be free from every imputation of guilt or blame, according to the sentiments of all the ancient philosophers'.[32] If suicide is criminal, he continues, it must be because it is a transgression of our duty either to God, our neighbour, or ourselves. These transgressions closely resemble those which, according to St Thomas Aquinas, are committed in committing suicide. Hume considers the three possible transgressions in turn. He first argues that suicide is not a transgression of duty to God. Everything that takes place in the universe, he says, is in accordance with the general laws and processes instigated by God. God governs everything by means of these general and immutable laws and all events are the action of the Almighty in the sense that they all proceed 'from those powers with which he has endowed his creatures'.[33] Within this general scheme 'men are entrusted to their own judgement and discretion . . . and may employ every faculty with which they are endowed, in order to provide for their ease, happiness, or preservation'.[34] From this and similar considerations Hume argues that everyone has 'the free disposal of his own life'.

He considers an objection to his argument. Can it be that human life is of such special importance that the Almighty has reserved to himself the sole right to dispose of it? But if this were the case it would be as wrong for us to *preserve* our lives as to *dispose* of them. 'If I turn aside a stone which is falling upon my head, I disturb the course of nature, and I invade the peculiar province of the Almighty by lengthening out my life beyond the period which by the general laws of matter and motion he had assigned it.'[35] He points out that a fly or an insect may destroy a human being. It would therefore be absurd to suppose that we should not be entitled to destroy what is dependent on such insignificant causes (i.e. destroy ourselves) and he therefore judges that 'When I fall upon my own sword, therefore, I receive my death equally from the hand of Deity as if it had proceeded from a lion, a precipice, or a fever'.[36]

It follows from what Hume is saying here that self-killings are as much under God's governance as any other act. But we should not accordingly assume that God ordains all particular acts, both good and evil, for Hume also maintains that Providence 'appears not immediately in any operation' and that 'Every event is alike important in the eyes of that infinite being, who takes in at one glance the most distant regions of space and remotest periods of time'. Thus, a self-killing, or any other act, is 'the action of the Almighty' only in that it is not a contravention of the laws of nature that control the universe. It is a product of the capacities with which human beings are endowed and is a part of the totality the deity is able to comprehend at one glance. But at the same time, Hume's God is not indifferent to human actions. The Almighty, Hume says, is displeased when we disturb society and we recognize this displeasure by 'the principles which he has implanted in human nature, and which inspire us with a sentiment of remorse if we ourselves have been guilty of such actions, and with that of blame and disapprobation, if we ever observe them in others'.[37]

Hume's response to the much-cited Socratic and traditional objection that one is placed by Providence like a sentinel at a particular station and should not desert it, is consistent with this view. He asks: '. . .why do you conclude that providence has placed me in this station? For my part I find that I owe my birth to a long chain of causes, of which many depended on the voluntary actions of man'. He argues that if it is Providence that has guided all these causes so that there is nothing in the universe that happens without its consent, then

> neither does my death, however voluntary, happen without its consent; and whenever pain or sorrow so far overcome my patience, as to make me tired of life, I may conclude that I am recalled from my station in the clearest and most express terms. 'Tis Providence surely that has placed me at this present moment in this chamber: but may I not leave it when I think proper, without being liable to the imputation of having deserted my post or station?[38]

8 HUME ON DUTIES TO OTHERS AND OURSELVES

When Hume turns to considering whether suicide is a breach of duty to one's neighbour and to society in general, he first makes the point that a man who retires from life does no harm to society; he merely ceases to do good. If he withdraws entirely, that is, if he ends his life, then he ceases even to receive benefits and so has no obligation to reciprocate. And even if we do feel bound in obligation, he says, even that obligation has limits: 'I am not obliged to do a small good to society at the expense of a great harm to myself; why then should I prolong a miserable existence, because of some frivolous advantage which the public may perhaps receive from me?' He enjoins us to consider circumstances in which his life is a burden to society or in which he hinders another person from being much more useful to society and says that 'in such cases my resignation of life must not only be innocent but laudable'.[39] And is not a tortured patriot, he asks, justified in killing himself in order not to divulge state secrets under torture? Here Hume is offering an argument of just the kind that Donne might have used in response to Aquinas's claim that suicide is wrong because it harms society. For Hume invokes that same principle – that society should not be harmed – to argue that suicide, under certain circumstances, would be entirely justifiable.

Lastly, Hume considers whether suicide is a transgression of duty to oneself. Certainly suicide is only consistent with duty to oneself, he concludes, when age, sickness or misfortune render one's life a burden. But he reminds us that people do not readily or easily consider self-destruction: 'such is our natural horror, of death, that small motives will never be able to reconcile us to it'. However, once existence is a burden we should rid ourselves of it, for "Tis the only way that we can be useful to society, by setting an example, which, if imitated, would preserve to every one his chance for happiness in life and would effectually free him from all danger or misery'.[40]

9   THE NEW STANDPOINT

Hume's defence of suicide is markedly different in tone from Donne's and it is conducted from a different point of view. The basis of Hume's defence is his certainty that the universe is as philosophy and science have said it is: a created and unified system, governed by immutable principles, within which human beings have disposal of their own lives. To suppose without proof or argument that within this system any special censures, privileges or exceptions apply to human beings is to fall prey to what Hume calls 'superstition'. The life of a man, he says, 'is of no greater importance to the universe than that of an oyster'.[41] At the same time, each one of us may lawfully employ that power with which nature has endowed us. Suicide, on this view, is not a breach of our duty to God because it is no more a disturbance of the laws of matter and motion than any other act it is in our power to perform. Hume remarks that it would be no crime (against God) to divert the Nile or the Danube from their courses if one had the power to. 'Where then', he asks, 'is the crime of turning a few ounces of blood from their natural channel?'[42]

When he elaborates, elsewhere in his writings, his moral philosophy, Hume argues that individuals stand in a relationship of reciprocity with society in general, receiving benefits for which they should reciprocate by furthering the interests of society. Our rules for living justly in society have their source, he says, in the natural sentiments or principles, referred to above, which, by agreement between people become transmuted into 'artificial' rules prescribing conduct that will benefit society as a whole and, thereby, benefit individuals also. For Hume there are no eternal and immutable moral laws, but only those that humankind living in communities generate from their natural sentiments. Thus, Hume's deity does not work directly or immediately in the world but only through the universal natural laws established from the beginning. Hume is therefore able to locate moral judgement firmly within the sphere of everyday human exchange and interaction without severing it completely from an anchorage in the purposes of the creator. He is also able to free himself to consider what, for him, are the central questions: does suicide constitute a failure of duty to our neighbours and society and to ourselves? This radical shift of viewpoint is made possible by the conception of God as creator of a law-governed, natural order. It allows Hume to abolish questions about the intrinsic rightness or wrongness of suicide and to consider its morality only by reference to the social and personal good or harm it produces. It means that Hume, unlike Donne, sees no need to meet claims to the effect that suicide is contrary to divine laws enunciated by revealed religion for, on his view, religion is natural rather than revealed. In a tersely-argued footnote to the essay on suicide he interprets Scripture in a way that is entirely consistent with everything he has proclaimed in his essay. He points out that not a single text of Scripture prohibits suicide and that Scripture 'has left us in this particular to our natural liberty', enjoining us to be submissive only to unavoidable ills. He deals very briskly with the sixth commandment, 'Thou shalt not kill', remarking that it is 'evidently meant to exclude only the killing of others over whose life we have no authority' and pointing out that magistrates modify this precept with reason and common sense in that they punish criminals capitally in spite of its injunction not to kill. In any case, he continues, 'all of the law of Moses is abolished, except so far as it is established by the law of Nature. And we have already endeavoured to prove that suicide is not prohibited by that law'. He points out that 'Christians and Heathens are precisely upon the same footing', meaning that the laws of nature are the universal source of the moral sentiments of all peoples, irrespective of their religious beliefs.[43]

Is Hume's defence of suicide a successful one? Certainly his account of natural law enables him to clarify and advance some of the claims that Donne struggled to validate; for by assuming a universal and undifferentiated causality he is able to dismiss as 'superstition' any qualms about special relationships or circumstances that might be thought to hold between human beings and Providence and that might affect our freedom to end our own lives when we choose to. In this way he strengthens the principle that Donne sought to establish: that of individual autonomy in the government of one's life. Even more importantly, he establishes the possibility of acts of suicide that are able to be rationally conceived and justified.

But Hume's views are not invulnerable to criticism. For from the view that suicide is to be judged right or wrong by reference to its aptness to yield benefit or harm it follows that a person without duties to society or family, and who, because of infirmity, no longer wishes to live, is justified in killing himself. And this ignores many considerations about the character of the person concerned and about the motives and intentions that might have prompted his suicide and that would generally be held to have bearing on the moral quality of his action. Hume emphasizes the consequential and societal aspects of morality at the expense of its personal and inward aspects. Moreover, the framework he sets up for his account of morality does not accommodate the principle that life is intrinsically valuable. Yet it is a principle that requires consideration in any adequate examination of the morality of suicide.

10 CLASSICAL UTILITARIANISM AND SUICIDE: BENTHAM AND MILL

Hume's essay on suicide was not officially published until 1773. It became an influential component of a body of material that constituted a rational defence of suicide and that had been issuing from writers such as Voltaire (1694–1778), Montesquieu (1689–1755), and Rousseau (1712–1778). Its moral theory was the precursor of the doctrine of utilitarianism that was propounded by Jeremy Bentham (1784–1832) and refined by John Stuart Mill (1806–1873). Hume, as we have seen, developed his theory from his account of natural law and human nature, arguing that our moral rules enshrine what he calls 'artificial virtues' that derive from natural sentiments. To explain this derivation he uses the notions of self-interest, sympathy and utility: we naturally desire our own good; we recognize or have an affinity with the feelings of others; and through this natural capacity for sympathy we have a concern to produce what is useful to the good of society and hence to ourselves, and so we devise rules, embodying 'artificial' virtues, to produce that good.

Jeremy Bentham's utilitarianism is somewhat differently grounded. He advances a psychological theory which asserts that human behaviour is governed by pain and pleasure and that each person acts to secure his or her own good. Added to this is a moral theory which holds that happiness, or pleasure, is the supreme good for humanity and that the aim of right action is to produce the greatest happiness of the greatest number. The juxtaposition of these two theories produces a conflict since, according to them, each of us is psychologically disposed to seek his or her own happiness but is morally required to produce the greatest good for everyone. Bentham therefore saw his task as one of reconciling individual interests with those of society by constructing a system 'the object of which is to rear the fabric of felicity by the hands of reason and law'.[44] Adopting Hume's term, he described the tendency in any act to produce happiness as its 'utility' and he used the principle of utility, or 'the greatest happiness principle', to judge and criticize social institutions and practices. His concern with human happiness was a secular one so his doctrine offers no religious foundation for the method he propounded. Moreover, he unashamedly included the pursuit of pleasure in his notion of happiness. He would have no truck with such abstractions as 'the welfare of the public' or 'the general interest' and adhered instead to the view that a society consists of its individual members and that its happiness is made up of the happiness of each member. At the same time he rejected moral doctrines that urged reliance, in making moral judgements, on one's own conscience or on a supposed moral sense and called for an 'external standard' by which to make such judgements. This external standard was, of course, the principle of utility. He required it to be employed in the administration of the criminal law as well as by individuals.

In the hands of John Stuart Mill the principle of utility, or greatest happiness, was explored and developed as a principle of individual morality. As proclaimed by Mill, utilitarian doctrine states that actions are right insofar as they produce happiness, wrong insofar as they produce the reverse of happiness. For him, as for Bentham, the rightness or wrongness of an action, and so of suicide, depends on its consequences. Again like Bentham, Mill does not ground his doctrine on religious beliefs, but he did think that the tenets of utilitarianism were entirely consistent with the ethics of Jesus of Nazareth and he said: 'whatever aid religion, either natural or revealed, can afford to ethical investigation, is as open to the utilitarian moralist as any other'.[45] He too rejected the idea of the individual conscience as a moral guide but at the same time held that one's conscience might be cultivated to develop a utilitarian sensibility.

11   CHANGES OF ATTITUDE

There are two particular aspects to eighteenth and nineteenth-century utilitarianism that must have strengthened the views of those who sought to free the act of self-killing from presuppositions of sin and crime. The first aspect belongs with the legal and social orientation that is characteristic of Bentham's utilitarianism. Bentham argued for a legal system in which punishment would be determined by the principle of utility. He was deeply opposed to Sir William Blackstone's *Commentaries on the Laws of England*, from which the remarks on self-homicide quoted at the end of Chapter One are taken, and he wrote a severe criticism of Blackstone in his *Fragment on Government*, first published in 1776. Had Bentham's proposals for reforming legislation been adopted in his own day the laws pertaining to suicide, as to many other matters, would probably have been changed in the early nineteenth rather than the mid-twentieth century and any moral and legal strictures on self-killing would have been determined by reference to the principle that 'it is the greatest happiness of the greatest number that is the measure of right and wrong'.[46] But Bentham's utilitarianism, although influential in that it was the subject of frequent and widespread discussion, was not taken with any real seriousness until the whole body of utilitarian doctrine, social, moral and political as well as legislative, had reached formidable proportions through the work of his followers. Even then, legislation concerning suicide changed very little although a slow shift in the public attitude was well under way early in the nineteenth century.

The second aspect of utilitarian thought that must have helped eventually to change attitudes to self-killing is the account of individual liberty propounded by John Stuart Mill. Mill maintained that the only good reason for exercising power over a member of a civilized community is to prevent harm to others. He wrote:

> His own good, either physical or moral, is not a sufficient warrant . . . the only part of the conduct of any one, for which he is amenable to society, is that which concerns others. In the part which merely concerns himself, his independence is, of right, absolute. Over himself, over his own body and mind, the individual is sovereign.[47]

Mill nowhere specifically discusses suicide so we have to try to infer from his argument in general what he might have said about it. His distinction between conduct that concerns others and conduct that concerns only oneself is a troublesome one. He recognizes this and expresses the objection that may be made to it: 'No person is an entirely isolated being; it is impossible for a person to do anything seriously or permanently hurtful to himself, without mischief reaching at least to his near connections, and often far beyond'.[48] His reply to the objection is that the sort of conduct that warrants interference by others is that which violates 'a distinct and assignable obligation to any other person or persons' or that disables a person 'from the performance of some definite duty incumbent on him to the public'. He continues:

> . . . with regard to the merely contingent, or, as it may be called, constructive injury which a person causes to society, by conduct which neither violates any specific duty to the public, nor occasions perceptible hurt to any assignable individual except himself; the inconvenience is one which society can afford to bear, for the sake of the greater good of human freedom.[49]

However, Mill at no point suggests that anyone should maintain a bland neutrality towards the actions of others. He advocates a complete freedom to voice moral approval or disapproval and, indeed, regards any such expressions, along with what he calls 'the *natural* penalties . . . falling on those who incur the distaste or the contempt of those who know them' as a powerful means of educating people towards social responsibility.

12   LIBERTY AND SUICIDE

Mill comes tantalizingly near the topic of suicide when, in discussing the application of his theory of liberty, he considers 'how far liberty may legitimately be invaded for the prevention of crime, or accident'. Concerning crime, he says: 'if a public authority, or even a private person, sees anyone evidently preparing to commit a crime, they are not bound to look on inactive until the crime is committed, but may interfere to prevent'.[50] Concerning accident he says,

If either a public officer or anyone else saw a person attempting to cross a bridge which had been ascertained to be unsafe, and there were no time to warn him of his danger, they might seize him and turn him back, without any real infringement of his liberty; for liberty consists in doing what one desires, and he does not desire to fall into the river. Nevertheless, when there is not a certainty, but only a danger of mischief, no one but the person himself can judge of the sufficiency of the motive which may prompt him to incur the risk; in this case, therefore (unless he is a child, or delirious, or in some state of excitement or absorption incompatible with the full use of the reflecting faculty), he ought, I conceive, to be only warned of the danger; not forcibly prevented from exposing himself to it.[51]

If we try to relate Mill's words on crime to suicide we see at once that they are, in that relationship, somewhat question-begging. For it is not entirely clear whether Mill did or did not view suicide as a crime. What we may infer from his views in general is that he would have regarded suicide as a matter that, for the most part, concerned only the individual but also as one that might be subject on occasion to disapproval. For it is arguable that he might have wanted to maintain that suicide and attempted suicide might sometimes violate 'a distinct and assignable obligation to an[y] other person or persons' and that they therefore warrant the intervention of authority in some way. His example of permissible intervention in what appears to be an imminent accident, as in the example of someone about to step on a dangerous bridge, tempts one to wonder what he would have said about intervention if the person approaching the bridge knew the danger and was intent on self-destruction. 'Liberty', Mill says, 'consists in doing what one desires' and from that it follows that one would be entirely justified in intervening in the case of someone who 'does not desire to fall into the river'. But what if someone *does* desire to fall into the river with the intent to die? Well, there are those words in parentheses in Mill's remarks, already quoted, that suggest he might regard it as proper to attempt to dissuade at least some cases of prospective suicides; for, whereas we may, according to Mill, merely give warning of the danger to a person who knows a risk and intends to take it, we may intervene more forcibly in the case of someone who is 'a child, or delirious, or in some state of excitement or absorption incompatible with the full use of the reflecting faculty'. Certain cases of prospective suicide might well fit or, at the very least, plausibly appear to fit one or other of those descriptions.

But even when qualified as above, does Mill's principle of individual liberty give us sufficient scope for intervening to deter a suicide to the extent to which most people, in following their moral intuitions, would want to? There must be very few people who would consider it morally acceptable to stand by and allow a suicide to take place (unless, possibly, it were that of some monstrously evil criminal) if they were in a position to prevent it. Yet Mill's account of individual liberty provides little scope for justifying intervention. Even if one is of the opinion that most people who embark on suicide do so irrationally, it follows from his view that once it is known that a prospective suicide is adult, rational and self-commanding in the ways specified by Mill, intervention should cease or should not be attempted. But this conclusion fails to recognize that a large part of what motivates the spontaneous, almost reflex, intervention on the part of a person suddenly confronted with what looks like the imminent suicide of another is not so much the thought that here is someone who may not have 'full use of the reflecting faculty' but that a portion of something valuable in itself, namely, life, is about to be destroyed. This is a separate and quite different kind of justification for intervening from the one based on the possibility of the suiciding person's being in an irrational state.

13   INADEQUACIES OF UTILITARIANISM

Utilitarian philosophers after Bentham and Mill rejected the view that happiness is the only intrinsic good and opted instead for a range of such values, including courage, friendship, beauty and health. More recently, in response to

criticisms about the difficulty of establishing an agreed body
of such values, another approach has been developed. This
newer approach has suggested that it is individual preferences
that have intrinsic value and utility consists in their satisfaction. But we need not engage here with the ramifications
and difficulties of these developments for they do not remedy
the inadequacies of utilitarianism as it relates to the issues of
suicide. Utilitarianism sees suicide as a moral issue only
insofar as its commission reduces the happiness of those
affected by it and leaves certain social and personal obligations
unfulfilled, and it is concerned with the consequences rather
than the nature of the act of suicide. Moreover, the scope
of utilitarianism's concern extends to none of the points at
which, in reflecting on suicide, one might wish to relate
one's present life in human society to any thoughts of what
might be beyond that present existence. Thus, the issues
that are of special importance in suicide and that induce the
greatest moral perplexity about it are precisely those that
utilitarianism disregards: the nature of the act of self killing;
its relation to one's thoughts about God and the sanctity
and meaning of life; and the significance of suicide as an act
that expresses one's moral character and passes a judgement
on life.

Something of the inadequacy of modern utilitarianism's
treatment of suicide is apparent in Jonathan Glover's book,
Causing Death and Saving Lives.[52] Writing from a predominantly utilitarian point of view, Glover finds only two
factors relevant to a decision about suicides. The person
contemplating it, he says, has two main questions to
consider. First, what would that person's future life be like,
and would it be worth living? Second, what effect would
his decision, either way, have on others.[53] He points out the
difficulties of dealing properly with the question about one's
future life, reminding us of the tendency of most prospective
suicides to close their minds to alternative courses of action
and to discussing the situation with friends or the Samaritans.
Predicting how one's life might or might not be changed
is, he says, always hard, unless one is incurably ill. He finds
the difficulty of deciding what sort of life is worth living
equally insurmountable, and he writes:

One test has to do with the amount of life for which you would rather be unconscious. Most of us prefer to be anaesthetized for a painful operation. If most of my life were on that level, I might opt for permanent anaesthesia, or death. But complications arise. It may be that we prefer to be anaesthetized for an operation only because we have plenty of other times to experience life without pain. It may be worth putting up with a greater degree of pain where the alternative is no life at all. And, even if we can decide about when we would rather be unconscious, the question whether a life is worth living cannot be decided simply by totting up periods of time to see if more than half our waking life is below zero in this way.[54]

When Glover turns to his second question, 'What effect would one's decision about suicide, either way, have on others?', he points out that a person's life might be so desperately bad that his or her interests should be put before those of any other person. But, he says,

sometimes an act of suicide can shatter the lives of others (perhaps parents) to a degree the person might never have suspected. Suicide cannot be seen to be the right thing to do without the most careful thought about the effects on all those emotionally involved. There is also the question of the loss of any general contribution the person might make to society.[55]

Perhaps the chief merit of these remarks is that they remind us of the difficulties of trying to envisage what the future might hold and of saying what sort of life is worth living. They do little more than broach one aspect of the morality of suicide, that of its consequences, and make no reference at all to the moral and metaphysical issues that are peculiar to suicide. Glover does not espouse the view that life is intrinsically valuable;[56] he is therefore confined to regarding life simply as a means to securing what *is* seen as intrinsically valuable and that, he points out, may vary considerably between persons. Moreover, his claim that the decision about suicide will depend in part on whether one's life is judged to be worthwhile suggests that he is committed to the view that only a worthwhile life merits being continued or saved. Glover says also that 'the moral question for the person contemplating suicide is simply whether his being dead would be a better state of affairs for himself or a worse one'.[57] This is a statement that has to be challenged; first, because it is difficult to make much sense of the thought that one might be 'better off dead' unless one has a secure belief in the survival of a self capable of being either better or worse off; second, because, as has already been argued, there is surely not just the one moral question about what state of affairs one's suicide might bring about but a number of moral questions, including those of the kind cited earlier in this section and that relate to the past as well as to the future.

14   SUICIDE AND THE LEGAL DEBATE

In Britain, the written laws pertaining to suicide were much the same in the early nineteenth century as when they were formulated in the medieval statutes. But their application, in general, was lenïent. The practice of burying a suicide at a crossroads with a stake through the heart seems to have been abandoned fairly early in the eighteenth century and the law authorizing the confiscation of a suicide's property was often circumvented by bringing a verdict of lunacy rather than *felo de se* on a person. But this leniency did little to change the deeply-entrenched legal point of view. In the sight of the law a suicide was either criminal and responsible, or insane and so not responsible, and many people continued to hold the view that any suicide must necessarily be insane. In either case the deed was stigmatized and the disrepute of the person concerned could be avoided only by casting doubt on whatever evidence there was to show that the death was indeed a suicide. Legal restrictions on the burial of suicides at crossroads were imposed in 1823 in England but this did little to change the climate of opinion and in 1854 attempted suicide was recognized as a crime. However, the law seems to have been applied to attempted suicides as leniently as it was to actual ones. The punishment imposed was left to the particular magistrate or judge dealing with a case and prison sentences mostly ranged from one to six months, the maximum sentence having been reduced to two years in 1882.

The gradual change to a non-punitive approach to suicide was probably advanced by a sociological study of it made by Émile Durkheim and published in 1897, though not translated into English until 1952.[58] Durkheim looked at suicide as a social phenomenon rather than a moral or criminal offence and decided that susceptibility to it depended on the degree to which a person is integrated into his or her society. He held that all societies have some kind of collective tendency towards suicide and that the strength of a society's tendency varied with the state of the society and was reflected in its members' individual propensities to the act. He drew attention to the fact that those who were closely integrated with social groups tended towards suicide far less than those who became isolated, and he distinguished three types of suicide: first, altruistic suicide, the self-killing undertaken by persons feeling themselves to be a burden on others, or by martyrs of one kind or another; second, anomic suicide, the self-killing of those affected by the weakening in a society of matrimonial, religious and general codes of conduct; and third, egoistic suicide, the self-killing undertaken by those who become isolated from social groups. This analysis, as it gradually became known, helped to detach suicide from the category of crime and enabled it to be considered alongside other social phenomena.

Change in official attitudes came very slowly. In the mid-twentieth century in Britain prison sentences were still being given to people found guilty of attempted suicide. In 1956, 559 persons were found guilty of attempted suicide and 37 of them were given sentences. However, in 1959, a study instigated by the then Archbishop of Canterbury and published under the title *Ought Suicide to be a Crime?*[59] recommended that attempted suicide should cease to be a crime, that the felony of suicide should be abolished and a new offence of aiding, abetting or instigating the suicide of another be created, and that there should be an alternative burial service for use in certain kinds of suicide. In 1961 an

Act of Parliament abolished the criminality of both attempted suicide and suicide. At the same time it was decided that aiding, abetting, counselling and procuring suicide should be considered separately. Charges could be brought against persons engaging in such activities, though only with the consent of the Director of Public Prosecutions, and the charge of manslaughter was made applicable only to the survivor of a suicide pact who had killed the other person or had been party to a third person's doing so.

During the nineteenth century another new perspective on suicide had been opened by investigation into the relationship between illness, or abnormality, and suicide. Some curious physiological theories were developed: that, for example, people with thick craniums tended to be suicidal and that the presence of phosphorus in the brain conduced to the act. But it was the development of psychiatric medicine, with its distinctions between psychosis and neurosis and its enquiries into abnormal personality and mental deficiency, that strengthened the belief, always present in the body of opinion about self-killing, that any and every suicide is necessarily mentally deranged and that eventually developed, in the twentieth century, into a fairly general view of the suicidal person as someone who is, in some sense, sick or ill or is, at the very least, in need of help. The underlying assumption of this attitude is that any person intending suicide should be deterred or restrained from carrying out her or his intention: the 'help' needed is help to refrain from the act. Writing in 1963, two years after suicide ceased to be a crime, Norman St John-Stevas expressed the attitude in the following way:

> The main need of those tempted to commit suicide is not legal punishment but help. Under the Mental Health Act of 1959 a doctor may order that an attempter be detained in hospital although there is no recording of any criminal conviction. The Act further provides for temporary committal to hospital. In both cases orders can only be made if the attempter is suffering from mental disorder, and may be a danger to himself or others. The only gap left by abolition of the criminal offence is that of a small suicidal minority,

uncertifiable but unwilling to accept treatment. They could
be dealt with by giving the courts power to make temporary
custody orders so that rehabilitation treatment could be
given.[60]

St John-Stevas also recommended that coroners should no
longer use the rider 'the balance of the mind was disturbed'
when giving a suicide verdict since the wording suggested
insanity, an imputation held to be damaging to relatives.

What might a dedicated defender of self-killing think of
this attitude to the matter? It replaces the view of the suicide
as some kind of lunatic with one that sees him as inadequate,
either emotionally, practically, intellectually or physically,
in the face of hardship or misery of some kind. It invites
the inference that the motive for abandoning the rider about
the balance of the mind being disturbed has almost everything
to do with sparing relatives damage and almost nothing to
do with trying to remove entrenched presuppositions about
a suicide's mental fitness. And at very best, it might be
argued, on this view the suicide is seen as a person needing
treatment or help; that is, help to draw back from what is
contemplated. It makes almost no allowance for a rationally-
conceived well-considered and non-desperate suicide of the
kind argued for by David Hume. On the other hand, the
view does encompass the very general perception of suicide
as, in most instances, the act of a person who is troubled
and distressed in the extreme and who therefore warrants
practical sympathetic attention from society. In refraining
from imputations of insanity it does provide some scope for
a more open consideration of suicide, and the Mental Health
Act of 1959, cited by St John-Stevas in the quoted passage
above, spreads a discreet safety-net for the rescue of those
who do not really want to take the leap they are desperately
heading for. There is also, in the view outlined, just a small
gap for the rationally-conceived suicide, since 'a small suicidal
minority, uncertifiable but unwilling to accept treatment'
escapes categorization by both the law and the Mental Health
Act.

15 CORONERS

In Chapter One it was mentioned that in the twentieth century coroners have become increasingly reluctant to record verdicts of suicide, that the law makes a strong presumption against suicide and that intention must be unequivocally established if a suicide verdict is to be brought. A report of a 1967 case states: 'Suicide is not to be presumed. It must be affirmatively proved to justify the finding. Suicide requires an intention', and in 1970 coroners were advised that 'there must be evidence that the deceased intended the consequences of his act'. The rigour of these injunctions is made clear in *Coroners' Inquiries: A Guide to Law and Practice* where we read:

> The need for proof of intent was seen by many coroners to be satisfied by the actions of the deceased. This may appear to be obvious, but the Divisional Court has been reluctant to accept that in a number of cases. Loading a gun, putting it to the head and pulling the trigger; standing on the railway line with arms outstretched in the path of an oncoming train, have both been rejected as evidence of intent to take one's own life.[61]

In 1970 a coroner who diverged from the spirit of this approach was sharply rebuked in the following terms:

> . . . this is really a plain case in which the coroner said that because there was no satisfactory evidence of accident, therefore it must be a case of suicide albeit there was no satisfactory evidence of suicidal intent. In my judgement that is a wrong approach to the matter and accordingly *prima facie* an order for *certiori* should go to quash the inquest.[62]

Since 1961 a small but significant change in the terminology used to speak of self-inflicted deaths has been taking place. The change is from describing such a death as 'committing suicide' to describing it as 'killing oneself'. The change has not yet spread very far beyond coroners' courts and in *The Law and Practice of Coroners* it is remarked that 'the public still refer to "committing" of suicide, although it has not been a crime for more than thirty years',[63] but in time the more neutral tones of the phrase 'killing oneself' should do much to detach the act from presuppositions of crime and sin even if, after reflection and discussion, grounds are established for according it, at any rate under some circumstances, moral censure of some kind.

In these last few paragraphs I have attempted a brief sketch of attitudes to suicide in Britain in the late twentieth century. By the twenty-first century a very different picture may be emerging. As the possibilities for prolonging life increase, considerations about the quality of individual lives may exercise the thoughts of people more than they do now. Faced, at the age of eighty, say, with the prospect of living for another forty years but with ever-diminishing capacities and scope for activity, a person might find reassurance in there being an option, with suitable safeguards, to arrange for the peaceful and untroublesome cessation of life before those further forty years had elapsed. Suicide, it has been suggested, could become a preferred mode of death: chosen, painless and dignified. This is a topic that will be returned to later.

NOTES

1 Donne, John (1984) *Biathanatos*, E. W. Sullivan II (ed.), University of Delaware Press.
2 Vaughan, William (1608) *The Golden Grove*, London, 2nd edn, Book I, Chapters XIV–XXIX.
3 Aristotle, *Nicomachean Ethics*, Book III, Chapter 7.
4 *Ibid.*, Book V, Chapter II.
5 Kant, I. (1930) *Lectures on Ethics*, Methuen, pp. 148–54. But Kant does not condone suicide. In his *Groundwork of the Metaphysics of Morals* (1785) he argues that to kill oneself is contrary to the moral imperative to 'act as if the maxim of your action were to become a universal law of nature', since it would be contradictory to go against a system of nature that functions to stimulate the furtherance of life.
6 Donne, John (1610) 'Pseudo-Martyr', quoted in *Biathanatos*, General Introduction, p. xi.

7 *Biathanatos*, p. 29.
8 Sprott, S. E. (1961) *The English Debate on Suicide*, Open Court, p. 25.
9 Donne, *op. cit.*, p. 35.
10 *Ibid.*, p. 36.
11 Holland, *op. cit.*, pp. 79–80.
12 Donne, *op. cit.*, p. 37.
13 *Ibid.*, p. 40.
14 *Ibid.*, p. 46.
15 *Ibid.*, p. 49.
16 *Ibid.*, p. 50.
17 *Ibid.*, p. 51.
18 *Ibid.*, p. 62.
19 *Ibid.*, pp. 62–3.
20 *Ibid.*, p. 64.
21 *Ibid.*, p. 68.
22 *Ibid.*
23 *Ibid.*, p. 71.
24 *Ibid.*, p. 72.
25 *Ibid.*, p. 75.
26 *Ibid.*, p. 84.
27 *Ibid.*, p. 115.
28 *Ibid.*, p. 116.
29 *Ibid.*, p. 128.
30 Hume, David, 'Of Suicide', in Singer, P. (ed.) (1986) *Applied Ethics*, Oxford University Press, pp. 19–27.
31 *Ibid.*, p. 20.
32 *Ibid.*
33 *Ibid.*, p. 21.
34 *Ibid.*, p. 22.
35 *Ibid.*, p. 23.
36 *Ibid.*, pp. 23–4.
37 *Ibid.*, p. 25.
38 *Ibid.*
39 *Ibid.*, p. 26.
40 *Ibid.*, p. 27.
41 *Ibid.*, p. 23.
42 *Ibid.*
43 *Ibid.*, p. 27.
44 Bentham, Jeremy (1789) *An Introduction to the Principles of Morals and Legislation*, J. H. Burns and H. L. A. Hart (eds), Methuen, 1982 edn, Chapter 1.
45 Mill, J. S. (1961) *Utilitarianism*, Fontana, 1962 edn, p. 273.

46 Bentham, Jeremy (1776) *Fragment on Government*, F. C. Montagne (ed.), Greenwood Press, 1980 edn, Preface, Section 2.
47 Mill, J. S. (1962 edn) *On Liberty*, Fontana, Chapter 1, p. 135.
48 *Ibid.*, p. 213.
49 *Ibid.*, p. 214.
50 *Ibid.*, p. 228.
51 *Ibid.*, p. 229.
52 Glover, Jonathan (1977) *Causing Death and Saving Lives*, Penguin.
53 *Ibid.*, p. 173.
54 *Ibid.*, p. 174.
55 *Ibid.*, p. 175.
56 *Ibid.*, p. 45.
57 *Ibid.*, p. 175.
58 Durkheim, Émile (1897) *Suicide*, Routledge & Kegan Paul, 1952 edn.
59 Church of England General Assembly Board for Social Responsibility (1959) *Ought Suicide to be a Crime?*, Church of England Information Office.
60 St John-Stevas, Norman (1963) *The Right to Life*, Hodder and Stoughton, p. 87.
61 Burton, J., Chambers, D. and Gill, P. (1985) *Coroners' Enquiries: A Guide to Law and Practice*, Klewer Law, pp. 82–3.
62 Knapman, P. and Powers, N. J. (1985), *The Law and Practice of Coroners*, B. Rose, p. 144.
63 *Ibid.*, p. 154.

CHAPTER THREE

Life, death and the absurd

1 SCHOPENHAUER ON SUICIDE

A nineteenth-century philosophy that provides a framework for reflecting on some of the issues neglected by J. S. Mill's utilitarianism is that of Arthur Schopenhauer (1788–1860). Schopenhauer became well-known in Western Europe in the latter half of the nineteenth century after the *Westminster Review* had published an article about him in 1853. That article was followed by others in French, German and Danish periodicals and the interest in Schopenhauer, along with translations of his work, spread rapidly. His philosophy took its impetus from Kant, 'marvellous Kant' as he called him.

Schopenhauer wrote a short essay on suicide, first published in 1851 in a volume of essays called *Parerga and Paralipomena*.[1] In the first part of the essay he propounds a point of view that looks as if it is entirely compatible with Mill's views on individual liberty. He deplores the fact that suicide is often regarded as a crime, 'especially in vulgar, bigoted England', and observes that most people tend to fulminate about it rather than argue against it. They declare that it is wrong, he says, 'whereas there is obviously nothing in the world over which every man has such an indisputable *right* as his own person and life'.[2] He suggests that we should consult moral feeling in order to decide about suicide, pointing out that if we learn that a friend has committed a crime such as murder, cruelty, fraud or theft, we feel resentment and desire punishment for the offender, but that if we hear of his voluntary death we are moved to a sorrow and sympathy that are often mingled with admiration for such courage. He reminds us that suicide was regarded by many Greeks and Romans, and by other cultures as well, as a noble death and he lavishly commends David Hume's essay on suicide as the most thorough refutation of the 'feeble sophisms' advanced by religion against self-killing. Christianity, he says, has at its core the truth that the real purpose of life is suffering. Since suicide is a rejection of suffering then Christianity must needs reject suicide. Antiquity, on the other hand, approved suicide because it rejected suffering. He maintains that mental suffering induces suicide more readily than physical suffering does and that as soon as the terrors of life outweigh the terrors of death people are prepared to end their lives. But the terrors of death are considerable and he remarks:

> Perhaps there is no one alive who would not already have made an end of his life if such an end were something purely negative, a sudden cessation of existence. But it is something positive, namely the destruction of the body, and this frightens people back just because the body is the phenomenon of the will-to-live.[3]

2   THE WILL-IN-ITSELF

The last phrase in that quotation – 'the body is the phenomenon of the will-to-live' – requires elucidation. It is the clue to the metaphysical basis of Schopenhauer's thought and to its capacity to engage with the issues of suicide that utilitarianism ignores. Without some understanding of that metaphysical basis, Schopenhauer's further remarks in his essay on suicide are enigmatic and appear to contradict much of what he has already maintained. For he goes on to say that suicide is 'opposed to the highest moral goal'[4] and that seen from a higher moral level it is a futile and foolish act.

Schopenhauer believed that his philosophy provided a key to ultimate truth. Its central concept is that of *will*. He held that the ultimate driving force and essence of the whole material world is will; not will thought of as one thinks of the purposeful will of an individual person, but as the blind impulsion of each thing to realize its own nature. Philosophical understanding, he maintains, consists in recognizing that, cosmically speaking, this is the way things are. The will that *is* the world he calls the will-in-itself.

Just as the world *is* the total will-in-itself, so, in Schopenhauer's scheme, is the human body an individual will. Thus, it is not that there is a physical world which becomes activated or driven by some separate force which is will: reality is one and it is will. Once a person has recognized that his will *is* himself, this understanding, Schopenhauer says,

> will become the key to the knowledge of the innermost being of the whole of nature. . . He will recognize that same will not only in those phenomena that are quite similar to his own, in men and animals, but continued reflection will lead him to recognize the force that shoots and vegetates in the plant . . . by which the crystal is formed . . . that turns the magnet to the North Pole . . . all these he will recognize as different only in the phenomenon, but the same according to their inner nature.[5]

Schopenhauer says that there is no explanation for will-in-itself. It is ungrounded, original and originating. It follows from this that there is no room in his philosophy for freedom of the individual will. For although I may, as an individual, cite reasons and motives for my actions, if I also acknowledge that I am ultimately part of the great unity of the will-in-itself, which is ungrounded and inexplicable, which simply *is*, then I have to acknowledge that what I actually will to do is fundamentally determined by what I am, whatever I am and however I have come to be what I am. In order to *do* something different I would have to *be* something different.

3 DENIAL OF THE WILL: SALVATION

There is a further aspect of Schopenhauer's thought that must be explained before his views on suicide can be understood. Although everything is ultimately will-in-itself, and although human beings are able, in certain ways, to have some insight into that ultimate condition, the usual and everyday manner in which we apprehend the world is simply as it appears to us in virtue of our intellectual equipment: we explain things by reference to causality, we reason about things by using concepts; more abstractly, we reason with mathematical ideas, and we also have a consciousness of ourselves as individuals that have particular wills. This is the familiar world of everyday and Schopenhauer, following Kant, calls it the world as it appears to us, or as we represent it to ourselves. But through our awareness of ourselves and others as individual aspects of will-in-itself we realize that everything is ultimately blind will, and although exhaustive knowledge of will-in-itself is not possible, we recognize, Schopenhauer says, that 'behind our existence lies something else, that becomes accessible to us only by our shaking off the world'.[6] Since the world is will and since each person, as a part of the world, is a part of that will, to shake off the world is to shake off one's will. Schopenhauer regarded this denial of will as the highest moral achievement and it is for this reason that, whilst maintaining in the essay on suicide that everyone has a right to end her or his own life, he also declares that 'suicide is opposed to the attainment of the highest moral goal since it substitutes for the real salvation from this world of woe and misery one that is merely apparent'.[7] The 'merely apparent' salvation that suicide secures is a release from one's particular portion of the ceaseless striving of will. Schopenhauer points out that this is a kind of contradiction since it is an instance of the will-to-live acting against itself. Because suicide is an act of will, it can never be a denial of will. Rather, it is the most flagrantly assertive manifestation of one's will to live. He writes: 'Just because the suicide cannot cease willing, he ceases to live; and the will affirms itself here even through the cessation of its own phenomenon, because it can no longer affirm itself otherwise'.[8]

Schopenhauer maintains that one way in which the real salvation that results from denial of one's will can be brought about is through suffering. But the suicide, weary with the wretchedness that makes him want to die, rejects his suffering by destroying his body. Schopenhauer likens him to 'a sick man who, after the beginning of a painful operation that could completely cure him, will not allow it to be completed, but prefers to retain his illness'.[9] He suggests that if only the prospective suicide would embrace his suffering he would be liberated from individual desires and strivings. They would become as nothing. For, since they are merely the will manifesting itself, when the will is denied they, too, disappear. In their place is the state of being of 'those who have overcome the world, in whom the will, having reached complete self-knowledge, has found itself again in everything, and then freely denied itself, and who then merely wait to see the last trace of the will vanish with the body that is animated by that trace'.[10] Those who have attained to denial of the will to live, Schopenhauer says, have experienced 'ecstasy, rapture, illumination, union with God'.[11]

Schopenhauer makes it clear that one cannot will to bring about the denial of one's will. The denial simply takes place at a point when a certain kind of illumination takes place. Will is then replaced by knowledge of the true nature of the world, so that a person perceives and contemplates that truth and is released from enslavement to the perpetual strivings of the individual will. When this occurs, he says, one is

> no longer the individual that knows in the interest of its constant willing . . . but the eternal subject of knowing purified of the will . . . And we know that these moments, when, delivered from the fierce pressure of the will, we emerge, as it were, from the heavy atmosphere of the earth, are the most blissful we experience. From this we can infer how blessed must be the life of a man whose will is silenced . . . Nothing can distress or alarm him any more; nothing can any longer move him; for he has cut all the thousand threads of willing which hold us bound to the world . . .[12]

In reaching this understanding of the nature of things there is a recognition of what Schopenhauer calls the futility of the individual will and an experience of the wholeness and totality of will-in-itself. For the person who has been considering suicide it nullifies the will to self-destruction and opens the way to 'the highest moral goal', the state in which the world as we ordinarily understand it is as nothing. Suicide has no place in Schopenhauer's 'higher morality'.

4 CRITICISMS AND COMMENTS

What happens to the ordinary world of 'representations' when will is denied? Schopenhauer's answer to that question follows from all he has maintained: the medley of desires, pleasures and pains constituting the world of representation becomes a nothingness, for that world *is* will and if will is denied then the denial constitutes 'the vanishing of the world, of its mirror'.[13] For those who are full of will the prospect of that nothingness is appalling, but for those who have denied will, Schopenhauer says, 'this very real world of ours with all its suns and galaxies, is – nothing'.[14]

Schopenhauer's metaphysical picture accommodates a number of our moral intuitions and moral experiences. It provides a way of thinking about what might lie 'behind our existence' and about our sense of the self and of its wilful egoism as that which prevents a person from achieving a true vision of the world and a peaceful unity with it. It also encompasses the kinds of issues relating to suicide that utilitarianism leaves untouched. It offers a way of thinking about the ultimate nature of things and about the relationship in which a transient human life may stand to any such ultimate reality. Moreover, Schopenhauer's account of the kind of change that takes place in a person when denial of the will occurs invites reflection on virtues and qualities that typify moral character: the abandonment of egoism; a feeling of affinity with others; and a sense of the possibility of experiencing and living in harmony with the inward nature of the world. He provides a metaphysical dimension for thought without reverting to a theological one and he draws attention to something already referred to more than once in this book, namely, the way in which the act of self-killing expresses a judgement on life.

Nevertheless, Schopenhauer's account presents us with formidable difficulties. For once we start thinking our way into the ramifications of his ideas we encounter some troublesome paradoxes. These paradoxes begin to show when we come to say such things as that it is only by, in some sense, losing the self that we find salvation. For what is it that is then saved if self, and so self-consciousness, are lost? Or perhaps we begin to think of a proper moral attitude as one that is somehow without will or desire. But how then are we to have goodwill towards others and to engage in moral actions if we are without will and are only contemplative of the world? If we adopt Schopenhauer's view, whatever our standpoint may be, the everyday world seems to have no ultimate meaning and ordinary human life appears pointless. Moreover, the 'salvation' that results from denial of the will seems to negate one's individuality so that it is difficult to understand how that salvation relates to one's personal existence; for the self that engages with the world has been abolished and the world itself is revealed as a meaningless flux. Is there then any point either to one's personal existence or to existence in general, and is there any reason why one should not commit suicide if one wishes to?

5   SUICIDE AND THE MEANING OF LIFE

The cast of mind that dwells on the thought that there is no ultimate meaning to existence was carefully investigated and developed in the first half of the twentieth century. Reflections on suicide had a prominent place in that enquiry. During the Second World War, Albert Camus (1913–1960) wrote a long essay which he called 'The Myth of Sisyphus'.[15] The English translation of it, first published in 1955, opens with these words: 'There is but one truly serious philosophical problem and that is suicide'. The problem, precisely stated, is that of giving an answer to the question

'Is life worth living?' For Camus, the seriousness of the question and of the philosopher's reply to it is judged by the actions entailed by them. He says: '. . . you can appreciate the importance of that reply, for it will precede the definitive act'. He maintains that the philosopher deserving of respect will 'preach by example'; that is, if life is deemed not worth living it will be ended.

Camus uses the terms 'the absurd' and 'absurdity' to describe what is experienced when we feel that life and the world are ultimately meaningless. He makes it clear that he is not going to offer a metaphysical argument to show that reality is fundamentally absurd. He takes it that most people experience absurdity and he therefore tries to describe what he calls 'an absurd sensitivity'. His interest is in the relationship between the self and suicide and in the exact degree to which suicide is a solution to the experience of absurdity. He points out that awareness of absurdity can spring into being in numerous ways. He writes:

> Great works are often born on a street-corner or in a restaurant's revolving door. So it is with absurdity . . . In certain situations, replying 'nothing' when asked what one is thinking about may be pretence in a man. Those who are loved are well aware of this. But if that reply is sincere, if it symbolises that odd state of soul in which the void becomes eloquent, in which the chain of daily gestures is broken, in which the heart vainly seeks the link that will connect it again, then it is as it were the first sign of absurdity.[16]

Camus writes, too, of the way in which the strange 'density' of the physical world evokes a sense of the absurd in us:

> The primitive hostility of the world rises up to face us across millennia. For a second we cease to understand it because for centuries we have understood in it solely the images and designs that we had attributed to it beforehand, because henceforth we lack the power to make use of that artifice. The world evades us because it becomes itself again . . . that denseness and that strangeness of the world is the absurd.[17]

The nullity of death is another indicator of the absurd for Camus:

> . . . in reality there is no experience of death . . . it is barely possible to speak of the experience of others' deaths. It is a substitute, an illusion, and it never quite convinces us . . . From this inert body on which a slap makes no mark the soul has disappeared. This elementary and definitive aspect of the adventure constitutes the absurd feeling. Under the fatal lighting of that density, its uselessness becomes evident.[18]

These quotations show that when Camus poses the question 'Is life worth living?' he is inviting reflection not so much on one's particular life as on life itself, on the way in which human beings relate to and exist in the world. What he wants to know is what kind of judgement on life the recognition of absurdity evokes. He asks: 'Does the Absurd dictate death?' and '. . . is there a logic to the point of death?'[19] He maintains that the horror of death becomes vivid only by reflecting on what he describes as 'the mathematical aspect of the event'. I take him to mean that it is only when I remind myself that I shall die at a particular time and place in the future, and that that time draws relentlessly nearer as each moment passes, that I begin to realize the inevitability of my own extinction. We experience the absurd when we realize the total absence of consciousness from a dead body and Camus wants to remind us of this realization, not so much in order to make us feel it all over again as to draw us back to the question he is raising: 'Is one to die voluntarily or to hope in spite of everything?'[20]

He reflects on how inadequate our knowledge is. In particular, we cannot know the *self*. Science, he says, in the end is metaphor and poetry, and although science permits us to 'seize phenomena and enumerate them', it does not enable us to 'apprehend the world'. Reason, classification and categories 'are enough to make a decent man laugh'.[21] Although self is something one is sure of, 'if I try to seize this self of which I feel sure, if I try to define and summarize it, it is nothing but water slipping through my fingers'.[22] He says that the absurd comes into being as the result of a confrontation between 'a bare fact and a certain reality'.[23]

The bare fact is that human beings yearn to find an ultimate meaning in things; the reality is that there is none. Absurdity springs into being when that yearning confronts what the world offers.

6   THE MYTH OF SISYPHUS

For Camus, absurdity is a fundamental truth that is symbolized in the mythical story of Sisyphus. Sisyphus was condemned by the gods to spend his time ceaselessly rolling a rock to the top of a mountain. Once at the top of the mountain the rock falls back to the bottom and Sisyphus rolls it up again. This futile labour was punishment for a number of impudent actions on his part. He had flouted many conventions, scorned the gods and had tried to cheat death. Camus looks upon him as the hero who epitomizes absurdity:

> one sees . . . the whole effort of a body straining to raise the huge stone, to roll it and push it up a slope a hundred times over . . . At the very end of his long effort measured by skyless space and time without depth, the purpose is achieved. Then Sisyphus watches the stone rush down in a few moments towards that lower world whence he will have to push it up again towards the summit.[24]

Camus says that what he is interested in is Sisyphus' consciousness of his plight when he makes those brief downward journeys to retrieve the stone. His consciousness of his situation makes him a tragic hero and he represents the modern condition. Camus remarks: 'If the descent is. . . sometimes performed in sorrow, it can also take place in joy'.[25] This is important for Camus since he detects a paradox in the experience of absurdity, a paradox in which we naturally seek to escape the very absurdity which we see as fundamental truth. Sisyphus, he feels, preserves the lucidity of this truth, acknowledges it, and knows that his fate belongs to him. He lives his absurdity and does not seek to escape it. His answer to the question 'Is one to die voluntarily or to hope in spite of everything?' is certainly not to commit suicide. But neither is it quite 'to hope in spite of everything'. Instead, it is to live in full knowledge of the pointlessness of the human situation, and to engage with and even enjoy what is before him.

7 TWO KINDS OF SUICIDE

Camus identifies two forms of escape from the truth of absurdity. One is physical, the other philosophical, or metaphorical, suicide. Philosophical suicide consists of a kind of intellectual abdication from confronting what is really the case; it escapes the lucid confrontation of absurdity by using absurdity as 'eternity's springboard'. It evades truth by taking the concept of absurdity and incorporating it into a further conception of reality that is able to include and make some sort of sense of this irrational element. Camus regards this as an insult to human reason which, although limited, has been the means of recognizing absurdity in the first place. Moreover, it deprives absurdity of its essential character of *opposition* to the human passion to understand the world. He regards the Danish philosopher, Kierkegaard (1813–1855), as the exemplification of this selling-out to the irrational. Kierkegaard, he says, wanted to escape 'the antinomy of the human condition'; he makes 'a leap of faith' and identifies absurdity with what is divine, thereby succumbing to the intense longing to find an explanation for things. Another form of philosophic suicide is to reject the fact that human reason is limited by denying that there are constraints upon it and by securing the solace of explanation through an unbridled intellectualism. Camus says: 'The abstract philosopher and the religious philosopher start out from the same disorder and support each other in the same anxiety. But the essential [for them] is to explain'.[26] The only way not to commit philosophical suicide is to hold fast to what one's limited reason has discovered, 'to be faithful to the evidence that aroused it'. That evidence is the absurdity engendered when our nostalgia for unity confronts the unyielding universe. Camus insists that this dislocation has to be lived with: 'Being able to remain on that dizzying crest – that is integrity and the rest is subterfuge'.[27] He holds that physical suicide is no more an appropriate response to absurdity than philosophical suicide is. It is just as much a consent and capitulation to absurdity as philosophical suicide is, since it is an acceptance of and a rushing forward to embrace one's future death rather than a living of the experience of absurdity. He started his enquiry in 'The Myth of Sisyphus' by asking whether life has to have a meaning in order to be lived but it now becomes clear, he says, that 'it will be lived all the better if it has no meaning'.[28] To commit physical suicide is to negate the human life that encounters absurdity when it demands, but does not receive, a rational response from the universe. Life has to be lived in order to keep absurdity alive and the only proper response to absurdity is rebellion. Of this rebellion Camus remarks: 'It is not aspiration, for it is devoid of hope. That revolt is the certainty of a crushing fate, without the resignation that ought to accompany it'.[29]

Camus, then, comes out against suicide because he sees it, in one way or another, as a capitulation or an escape from the reality of absurdity. But, he says, 'the absurd does not liberate; it binds'. Absurdity binds because it makes us recognize that the fact of death destroys any possibility of arriving at 'that freedom to be, which alone can serve as basis for a truth'.[30] At the same time, the recognition that there is no eternal life releases 'the absurd man' from the hope of a higher freedom, from the constraint of thinking that there might be some meaning that will shape a person's life and that must be taken seriously:

> . . . the absurd man realizes that hitherto he was bound to that postulate of freedom on the illusion of which he was living. In a certain sense, that hampered him. To the extent to which he imagined a purpose to his life, he adapted himself to the demands of a purpose to be achieved and became the slave of his liberty.[31]

8   THE FRAMEWORK OF CAMUS'S THOUGHT

The framework that Camus sets himself to work within is not that of strict philosophical argument. He does not, as we have seen, purport to offer a metaphysical argument to show that ultimately reality is absurd. Instead, his appeal is to what he takes to be a fairly widespread experience, that of being unable to find a meaning for life and the universe. The anchorage for his enquiry is his own self-awareness and his capacity to reason. He uses his self-awareness to check the tendency of reason to think it can know more than it actually is able to, and also constantly to remind himself of the lucid conception – so easily evaded or escaped by either physical or mental suicide – of the absurdity of the human situation. What Camus's thought is exhibiting here is the slow but massive shift from the emphasis of earlier centuries on a consciousness that had, with different weightings at different times, divine and religious and social authority as its dominant contents, to a consciousness that was gradually becoming more and more an awareness of the individual self, and of its mode of existence as of the utmost significance in any attempt to understand reality. Camus sees that human reason cannot secure knowledge of God. He finds the world as present to us incorrigibly and impenetrably meaningless and he therefore develops his enquiry from what he feels sure of: his own life. This is the basis of the morality that he carves out from his investigation into the truth of the relationship in which human beings stand to life. Suicide, physical or philosophical, is a deviation from or corruption of that truth. Since there is no meaning in things then everything in the world is on the same level. There is no future and no hope, only life now and death which is 'there as the only reality'.[32] What has to be resisted is the intellectual or emotional creation of an illusion of some kind of freedom. What has to be embraced is the picture of 'a burning and frigid, transparent and limited universe in which nothing is possible but everything is given, and beyond which all is collapse and nothingness'.[33] And what Camus wants to know, in the face of this nothingness, is 'whether or not one can live *without appeal*'; that is, whether it is possible to live in a full awareness of the pointlessness of existence or whether the reasonable consequence of confronting absurdity might be to end one's absurd life.

It is of supreme importance to Camus that the truth of

absurdity is clearly perceived at all times and he maintains that it is an attitude of revolt or rebellion that keeps alive a person's sensibility to the absurd. His reasoning seems to be along the following lines. If an earthly life is all we have, and if the truth of the human condition is that life is absurd, then we can only live that life fully by retaining a perpetual consciousness of that truth. One way of keeping one's sense of absurdity alive is to be constantly throwing oneself against it in every possible way, thereby perpetuating experience of its stubborn senselessness as the climate of every aspect of one's existence. This is an acceptance of absurdity but not a capitulation to it. But Camus's reasoning here is less than strict. Rebellion certainly is not deducible from his premises about absurdity. But he does seem to recognize this, for he writes, 'One of the only coherent philosophical positions is . . . revolt'.[34] What he has actually done, on the basis of his insights, is to make certain fundamental choices. He has opted for the values of truth and a full life and has seen rebellion rather than reconciliation or quietism as a truthful response to absurdity; one moreover that will extend one's consciousness of it so that fullness of life is achieved.

9   REBELLION AND TRUTH

To develop his view that rebellion is the way to keep faith with absurdity, Camus sketches examples of rebellious lives; those of the lover, the actor, the adventurer. But he insists that any life can be lived in awareness of the absurd; 'equally well, if he wishes, the chaste man, the civil servant, or the President of the Republic'.[35] But the most gloriously absurd life is, he says, that of the absurd creative artist. It is a kind of double living because it is a re-creating of what one finds, a describing and not an explaining of it. Yet it is not an *escape* from absurdity. It is itself absurd in that 'it makes the mind get outside of itself and places it in opposition to others, not for it to get lost but to show it clearly the blind path that all have entered upon'.[36] The absurd work of art is a kind of repudiation of all the constructions and explanations a creative artist might be tempted to impose on things. It simply multiplies appearances and images and so commands the kind of close attention that can comprehend absurdity. Camus says: 'If the world were clear, art would not exist'.[37]

He takes Dostoevsky as an example of a great novelist who is also a philosophical novelist, not in the sense that he has some 'thesis' to present but insofar as he does not yield to the temptation to create illusions and hopes. Dostoevsky's characters are much concerned to ask questions about the meaning of life and in his *Diary of a Writer* he ponders the reasoning that arrives at what he describes as 'logical suicide'. In the *Diary* we read:

> Since in reply to my questions about happiness, I am told, through the intermediary of my consciousness, that I cannot be happy except in harmony with the great all, which I cannot conceive and shall never be in a position to conceive . . . I condemn that nature which, with such impudent nerve, brought me into being in order to suffer – I condemn it to be annihilated with me.[38]

The mood here is of a bitter and profoundly angry defiance. Camus compares it with the attitude of another Dostoevskian character, Kirilov, in *The Possessed*. Kirilov, he says, feels that God must exist but he knows that he does not and cannot exist and he regards this as a sufficient reason for a suicide that will be an assertion of his rebellion and new-found liberty. In the novel Kirilov maintains that 'If God does not exist, I am god'.[39] He does not mean that if God does not exist he himself is therefore an immortal and all-powerful deity, but that he has dominion over his own life; there are no absolute moralities which he is commanded to discover and obey, no God whose will must be followed.

But why does Camus seem to accept that Kirilov's suicide is somehow sublimely apt when he has condemned suicide in general as by no means an appropriate response to the realization of absurdity? The only answer to that question is, it seems, that Camus is somewhat ambivalent about the philosophy implicit in Dostoevsky's novels. Kirilov, he points out, recognizes that his liberty should really lead to a celebration of life, for in the novel he says, 'If you feel *that* [meaning the freedom he has now recognized] you are a Czar and, far from killing yourself, you will live covered with glory'.[40] Nevertheless, he *does* kill himself, 'out of love for humanity', Camus says, for 'he feels he must show his brothers a royal and difficult path on which he will be the first'.[41] Yet Kirilov does not wish others to follow him by killing themselves but by becoming enlightened, so that 'this earth will be peopled with Czars and lighted up with human glory'.[42] In a later novel, *The Brothers Karamazov*,[43] Dostoevsky makes the move that Camus has described as philosophical suicide. He takes what Camus sees as an irrational leap from living with absurdity to a Christian belief in immortality. Camus writes: 'What contradicts the absurd in that work is not its Christian character but rather its announcing a future life'.[44] Dostoevsky, like Kierkegaard, has encompassed rather than confronted absurdity, using it as the basis of a hope for a meaningful future. That is something that would never be attempted in a genuinely or wholly absurd work of art.

10 THOMAS NAGEL AND THE ABSURD

A somewhat different approach to the topic of absurdity is made by the American philosopher, Thomas Nagel, in a paper published in 1971.[45] Nagel bases his analysis of the absurd on an everyday understanding of the word. He says:

> In ordinary life a situation is absurd when it includes a conspicuous discrepancy between pretension or aspiration and reality: someone gives a complicated speech in support of a motion that has already been passed; a notorious criminal is made president of a major philanthropic foundation; you declare your love over the telephone to a recorded announcement; as you are being knighted, your pants fall down.[46]

On this account the absurd is seen as a species of comic incongruity between different elements of experience. At a philosophical level Nagel regards it as a similar kind of incongruity or clash between the seriousness with which we take our lives and 'the perpetual possibility of regarding everything about which we are serious as arbitrary or open to doubt'.[47] He maintains that the propensity to take our lives seriously and the capacity to step back and survey that seriousness are simply facts about human beings, and that absurdity consists in the further fact that we are able to take that external view of ourselves, recognizing the arbitrariness of all we do, without ceasing to engage seriously with life.

Nagel is critical of Camus's analysis of absurdity as arising because the world fails to meet our demands for meaning. It suggests, he says, that those demands might be met if the world were different. But if we think about this we see that whatever we may think of to furnish a meaning for the world can be doubted: our doubts are simply pushed back a further step. From this he concludes that absurdity cannot arise from the world's failure to meet our demand for meaning but from the collision within us of the two standpoints already described. He points out that one way to avoid absurdity would be to sacrifice our capacity for self-consciousness and self-transcendence. This is not something we can just decide or will to do however. Another way of avoiding absurdity might be, he says, to try to abandon one's individual and earthly existence, endeavouring to 'identify as completely as possible with that universal viewpoint from which human life seems arbitrary and trivial': the practice of some oriental religion might go some way towards effecting this kind of avoidance of the absurd. Nagel says that the final escape is suicide. But this is not a solution he seems to want to consider. He is more concerned with diluting the intensity and drama with which Camus, he thinks, has infused our perceptions of absurdity: as if it were a problem 'to which some solution must be found – a way of dealing with prima facie disaster'.[48] He regards Camus's advocacy of rebellion as 'romantic and slightly self-pitying' and maintains that our absurdity warrants neither distress nor defiance to any great extent. He advises that we approach our lives with irony rather than with heroism or despair.

What is chiefly of interest in all of this for our present purposes is the difference between the responses given by Camus and Nagel to their experiences of reflecting on human life in a cosmic setting. Even their analyses of absurdity, although they have common elements, have different emphases and express different attitudes. Camus is disappointed and made rebellious by the intractable and unyielding opaqueness of things. He comes to the world expecting to find somewhere in it a richness of meaning which, even if not absolute, can give human life some significance and appease what he calls his 'appetite for unity'. But the more he searches the more he finds only the blind pointlessness of existence. He recognizes he is on his own, that nothing in the world will declare a meaning or value for the world and that he must therefore decide its worth for himself. Hence the challenge with which he begins *The Myth of Sisyphus*: 'There is but one truly serious philosophical problem and that is suicide. Judging whether life is or is not worth living amounts to answering the fundamental question of philosophy'.[49] Nagel, in contrast, when he takes the transcendental step to review the human situation, perceives a comic aspect to our Sisyphean plight. And for him, absurdity is something to be adapted to rather than be scornful of. It is not a problem but simply a fact to be recognized; and certainly not one that should generate any serious considerations of suicide. Our ability to transcend ourselves in thought should, he suggests, enable us to see our limitations and help us to appreciate what he describes as 'the cosmic unimportance of the situation'. If it is the case that nothing matters ultimately then we can 'approach our absurd lives with irony instead of heroism or despair'.[50]

Because Nagel emphasizes the comic element in the absurd and derives his philosophical concept of absurdity from comic or embarrassing situations he is able to disparage the tragic and challenging aspects of it that are perceived by Camus. Were he to consider that sense of the absurdity of life that is generated when a person of burgeoning talent is struck down by a freakish accident or when children in one continent starve while expensively-maintained food 'mountains' accumulate in another, his recommendation of irony as a response to absurdity would show up as inadequate. Leaving aside the thought that it would be extremely tedious to be part of a human race whose members were striving to be uniformly ironic about the unfathomableness of reality, one would surely expect, hope for and welcome a wide range of responses to the experience of absurdity, not only among people in general but also in each particular individual, depending on his or her current circumstances. For sometimes the intractable absurdity of the human situation crushes us with its blind senselessness, sometimes it delights and liberates us, and sometimes it invokes only indifference. Camus recognized this when he remarked that Sisyphus' descent is sometimes performed in sorrow but that 'it can also take place in joy'. In fact, his approach is by no means as gloom-laden as Nagel seems to think it is. Camus writes:

> Happiness and the absurd are two sons of the same earth. They are inseparable. It would be a mistake to say that happiness necessarily springs from the absurd discovery. It happens as well that the feeling of the absurd springs from happiness . . . One must imagine Sisyphus happy.[51]

It is, then, a failing of Nagel's account that it seems to suggest that it would be rational and commendable to protect oneself by means of irony from both the depths and heights of feelings explored by writers such as Dostoevsky, Tolstoy, Kafka and many other creative artists and, if possible, from real-life experiences of an exalted or harrowing kind. One might also infer from his account that it would be advisable ironically to temper our dreams, aspirations, visions and imaginative activity in general. But how, then, would one develop the capacity to respond to the range of feelings and experiences encountered in life? And would one be able to acquire the kind of sensibility that could understand the inward aspect of suicide? Would suicide be regarded merely as a lapse from the virtue of irony?

NOTES

1 Schopenhauer, Arthur, 'On Suicide', in his (1974) *Parerga and Paralipomena*, vol. II, Oxford University Press.

2 *Ibid.*, p. 306.

3 *Ibid.*, p. 310.

4 *Ibid.*, p. 309.
5 Schopenhauer, Arthur (1818) *The World as Will and Representation* (2 vols), E. F. J. Payne (trans.), Dover, 1966 edn, vol. I, pp. 109–10.
6 *Ibid.*, p. 405.
7 *Ibid.*, p. 309.
8 *Ibid.*, p. 399.
9 *Ibid.*
10 *Ibid.*, p. 411.
11 *Ibid.*, p. 410.
12 *Ibid.*, p. 390.
13 *Ibid.*, p. 410.
14 *Ibid.*, pp. 411–12.
15 Camus, Albert (1975) *The Myth of Sisyphus*, Penguin, p. 11.
16 *Ibid.*, p. 19.
17 *Ibid.*, p. 20.
18 *Ibid.*, p. 21.
19 *Ibid.*, p. 16.
20 *Ibid.*, p. 22.
21 *Ibid.*, p. 26.
22 *Ibid.*, p. 24.
23 *Ibid.*, p. 33.
24 *Ibid.*, p. 108.
25 *Ibid.*, p. 109.
26 *Ibid.*, p. 48.
27 *Ibid.*, p. 50.
28 *Ibid.*, p. 53.
29 *Ibid.*, p. 54.
30 *Ibid.*, p. 56.
31 *Ibid.*, p. 57.
32 *Ibid.*, p. 56.
33 *Ibid.*, p. 58.
34 *Ibid.*, p. 53.
35 *Ibid.*, p. 84.
36 *Ibid.*, p. 88.
37 *Ibid.*, p. 90.
38 Dostoevsky, F. (1873–81) *The Diary of a Writer*, Boris Brasel (trans.), Ianmead edn, December 1876 entries.
39 Dostoevsky, F. (1953) *The Devils*, Penguin.
40 Camus, *op. cit.*, p. 98.
41 *Ibid.*, p. 99.
42 *Ibid.*
43 Dostoevsky, F. (1969) *The Brothers Karamazov*, Penguin.

44 Camus, *op. cit.*, p. 102.
45 Nagel, Thomas, 'The Absurd', reprinted in Hanfling, O. (ed.) (1987) *Life and Meaning*, Blackwell.
46 *Ibid.*, p. 51.
47 *Ibid.*
48 *Ibid.*, p. 58.
49 Camus, *op. cit.*, p. 11.
50 Nagel, *op. cit.*, p. 59.
51 Camus, *op. cit.*, pp. 110–11.

CHAPTER FOUR

Existentialism and suicide

1 FROM ABSURDITY TO EXISTENCE

Camus wanted to find out if life in general is worth living. He felt that if it were not worth living then one would be justified in committing suicide. He discovers no meaning to life; it has a Sisyphean pointlessness. Yet he judges life worthwhile in that it is able to become a celebration of the absurdity that is its ultimate nature. He points out that a lucid recognition of absurdity liberates us from false hopes and from rationalizations about the meaning of life. He rejects suicide because it ends all possibility of maintaining one's awareness of absurdity and he regards both physical and philosophical suicide as evasions of confrontation of the truth. He argues that rebellion rather than capitulation is the way to keep the truth of absurdity alive. His overriding interest is in the relationship between the self and suicide and Camus's supreme value is a person's continuing awareness of absurdity. One's individual life is worthwhile when it realizes the possibility offered by life itself; that is, when it is lived with a vivid consciousness of absurdity.

Camus's thought developed something begun by Schopenhauer: the focusing of attention on the individual's experience of existence. As the focus sharpened, personal existence and the relationship in which a human being stands to the world, rather than to traditional moralities, became influential in guiding reflection about suicide and forming views on the human life. Camus, it has been pointed out, did not provide a philosophical framework for his thought and never intended to do so. But his contemporary, the French philosopher, Jean-Paul Sartre (1905–1980), became a major exponent of the philosophy of existentialism and pursued interests similar to those of Camus. He used the concept of absurdity, though somewhat differently from Camus, and by means of a detailed analysis of the nature of human existence provided philosophical grounds for a perspective on life and death that had previously been expressed in literature and the other arts but not systematically articulated in philosophy.

Existentialism covers a wide range of views but, however broad its scope, it is always rooted in the experience of what it is like to exist as a human being. Its investigations are in one sense deeply personal in that they are about the structures and conditions of the personal existence of every human being. It works to give an account of the individual's consciousness of existence and from this concern flow its main pre-occupations: questions about freedom, action, choice, personal authenticity, relationships with the world and other people, and with the ways in which our values are derived from our consciousness of personal existence.

A short extract from Jean-Paul Sartre's novel, *The Reprieve*, will convey the style and mood of existential awareness. In the novel a man called Mathieu, in the tense days just before the outbreak of the Second World War, is contemplating suicide. He is experiencing a profound sense of the meaning-less of the outer world of things and an emptiness within himself:

> Half-way across the Pont-Neuf he stopped and began to laugh: liberty – I sought it far away: it was so near that I can't touch it, it is, in fact, myself. I am my own freedom. He had hoped that one day he would be filled with joy, transfixed by a lightning-flash. But there was neither lightning-flash nor joy: only a sense of desolation . . . He reached out his hands and slid them slowly over the stone parapet, it was wrinkled and furrowed, like a petrified sponge, and still warm from the afternoon sun. There it lay: a plenitude. *He longed to clutch that stone, and melt into it, to fill himself with its density and repose.* But there was no help in it: it was outside, and forever. There lay his hands on the

white parapet, bronze hands, they seemed, as he looked at them. But, just because he could look at them, they were no longer his . . . He closed his eyes and they became his own again . . . My hands: the inappreciable distance that reveals things to me, and sets me apart from them forever. *I* am nothing; *I* possess nothing. As inseparable from the world as light, and yet exiled, gliding like light over the surface of stones and water, but nothing can ever grasp me nor absorb me. Outside the world, outside the past, outside myself: freedom is exile and I am condemned to be free.

He walked on a few steps, stopped again, sat down on the parapet, and watched the river flowing past. What shall I do with all this freedom? . . . Shall I take the train? What did it matter? − go, or stay, or run away − acts of that kind would not call his freedom into play. And yet he must risk that freedom. He clutched the stone with both hands and leaned over the water. A plunge, and the water would engulf him, his freedom would be transmuted into water. Rest at last − and why not? This obscure suicide would also be an absolute, a law, a choice, and a morality, all of them complete. A unique, unmatchable act, a lightning-flash would light up the bridge and the Seine. He need only lean a little further over, and he would have made his choice for all eternity. He leaned over, but his hands still clutched the stone, and bore the whole weight of his body. Why not? He had no special reason for letting himself drop, nor any reason for not doing so. And the act was there, before him, on the black water, a presentiment of his future. All hawsers cut, nothing now could hold him back: here was his freedom, and how horrible it was! Deep down within him he felt his heart throbbing wildly: one gesture, the mere unclasping of his hands, and I would have been Mathieu. An effluence from the river bemused his senses: sky and bridge dissolved: nothing remained but himself and the water: it heaved up to him and rippled around his dangling legs. The water, where his future lay. At the moment it is true, I'm going to kill myself. Suddenly he decided not to do it. He decided: it shall merely be a trial. Then he was again upon his feet and walking on, gliding over the crust of a dead star. Next time, perhaps.[1]

That passage contains many characteristics typical of existential sensibility: a sense of solitariness, alienation, and lack of meaning; of the strangeness of matter and things; of the apparent contingency and pointlessness of life; of one's inward self as a kind of nothingness that longs to exist as an incorrigibly real being that has both physical presence and meaning; of the anguish of recognizing that human freedom is total but also meaningless because, in the end, there is nothing, neither grounds nor reasons, to determine one's choices of actions and values. But Mathieu's thoughts as he stands on the Pont-Neuf are not simply expressions of his particular mood of despair and desolation. According to Sartre they reveal the underlying structure not only of Mathieu's own existence but of the existence of every human being. Sartre does not explicitly discuss this structure in his novels, although many of them vividly exemplify it. His full philosophical account is in *Being and Nothingness*, a large work published in 1943.[2] Once we know the philosophical underpinning of Mathieu's experience, every phrase of his reflections acquires additional significance. But before turning to that underpinning there are details of Mathieu's thoughts about suicide to be considered.

2 EXISTENTIAL FREEDOM

Mathieu's thought that he might throw himself over the bridge does not arise immediately from a despair over some particular events or circumstances of his life. What has happened is that he has come to a realization about his personal freedom. He had, he says, 'sought it far away', but now he recognizes that it is so near to him that he cannot even touch it: 'it is, in fact, myself'. The realization, unexpectedly, is not a joyous one and for the moment we are not told what he means in saying that his freedom is 'himself'. But we begin to discover something of his meaning from his reflections on the experience he is undergoing. He senses the massive solidity of the stone bridge and sees his own hands lying on its parapet as if they are somehow not parts of *him*. Only on closing his eyes do the hands seem to belong to him again. That central 'him' that feels the presence of the bridge and sees the hands on the parapet seems to be unable to make proper contact with anything it experiences: 'He longed to clutch to that stone, and melt into it, to fill himself with its density and repose. But there was no help in it: it was outside and forever.' A little later Mathieu says 'I am nothing; I possess nothing . . . nothing can ever grasp me or absorb me'. This total exclusion of himself, of his interior being, from all that is present to him constitutes, he now sees, the freedom he has sought. Freedom, he says, 'is exile'. He decides that this alienation renders him accountable to no one. He is devoid of any purpose, and although he might still go to the railway station, take the train to Nancy and join the men already mobilized, or might run away, or stay where he is, he recognizes that no act of that kind would 'call his freedom into play'. He wants to test his freedom and since his freedom is, he now realizes, his own existence, he can risk it only by risking his life. He sees that he is free even to kill himself if he so chooses, and that freedom is terrifying because there is no reason why he should kill himself and no reason why he should not: he has to choose what he will do on the basis of nothing. That is what his freedom means. Thus he leans over the bridge and comes to the point of saying: 'At the moment *it is true*, I'm going to kill myself'.

In all this, Mathieu is not simply manifesting a certain kind of mood or attitude towards life. What he is coming to understand, according to Sartre's view, is something about the structure of his own existence and of every human life, namely, that there is a fundamental freedom that is ultimately unavoidable and which is the very condition of being a human being. What is now important for him is that having understood what his freedom is he should exercise it. His deep concern is not about *what* he will do but that whatever he does it shall be the outcome of his free choice and be undertaken in awareness of what his freedom means and so be an authentic act. Suicide does not present itself to him either as something intrinsically good or bad, nor as something that might have good and bad consequences; nor does he think about any duties or obligations he has. Suicide is the ultimate challenge to the freedom the nature of which he has just discovered. If he did choose to kill himself his suicide, he says, would be 'an absolute, a law, a choice, and a morality'.[3]

3 THE PHILOSOPHICAL UNDERPINNING

Sartre's fundamental philosophical question is: What is it like to be a human being? His answer is already encapsulated in the title of his book, *Being and Nothingness*. He maintains that we have two modes of being in the world which together make up what he calls 'human-reality'. Human-reality consists of being and of nothingness and he has special terms for these two modes of existence: Being–in–itself, which is the mode of existence of an object or thing, and Being-for-itself, which is the mode of existence of consciousness. When Mathieu regards his hands lying on the parapet of the Pont-Neuf he is vividly aware of them simply as bits of matter, meaningless objects belonging with everything that is 'outside'. They are In-itself. He feels set apart from them by his consciousness of them. And of his consciousness itself he says: '*I* am nothing. *I* possess nothing. As inseparable from the world as light, and yet exiled, gliding like light over the surface of stones and water, but nothing can ever grasp *me* nor absorb *me*' (my emphases). This ungraspable nothing, Mathieu's consciousness, is a For-itself.

Sartre describes the existence of the In-itself, or a phenomenon or thing, as 'opaque to itself . . . because it is filled with itself'. A thing has no consciousness of itself; it just exists. He says '. . . the In-itself has nothing secret; it is solid [*massif*] and there is not the slightest emptiness in being, not the tiniest crack through which nothingness might slip in'.[4] In contrast, the For-itself, or consciousness, has no such fullness of existence; it is no-*thing*. In being conscious it never regards itself as a thing but only as not that thing of which it is conscious. For Sartre, to be a human being is to exist as both a consciousness and a thing, as a For-itself and an In-itself. He asks: 'What is the meaning of that being which includes within itself these two radically separated regions of being?'[5]

Sartre's answer to his own question is that freedom is the meaning of human existence. The human being is both a thing (an In-itself), and a consciousness (a For-itself) and this dual mode of existence is at once the condition of human freedom and what constitutes human meaning. He says: '. . . there is no difference between the being of man and his *being free*'.[6] When Mathieu finds his freedom within himself – so near to him that he cannot touch it – it is this that he recognizes. Freedom is the nothingness we experience when we are conscious of what we are not. It makes us aware of the possibility of choosing what we will be in the future. Mathieu sees suicide not only as a possibility for his future action but also as a way of ending the freedom which he cannot escape as long as he is alive.

Both in his novels and his philosophical writing, Sartre argues his analysis of human-reality by means of detailed descriptions of vivid personal experiences of what it is like to exist as a human being. He uses numerous examples which exhibit that sense of a bifurcation between the multitude of things, including one's own body, that make up the phenomenal world and one's consciousness *of* all those things. In the novel *Nausea*,[7] the main character, Antoine Roquentin, in a series of strange episodes, becomes fearfully aware of the overwhelming presence and density of physical objects and of the strangely dislocated nature of his own experience. Standing on the seashore, he picks up a pebble and is sickened and horrified by its stubborn and overwhelming existence. Later, in reflecting on the incident, he says:

> Objects ought not to *touch* . . . But they touch me, it's unbearable . . . Now I see, I remember better what I felt the other day on the sea-shore, when I was holding that pebble. It was a sort of sweet disgust. How unpleasant it was . . . a sort of nausea in the hands.[8]

The feeling of dislocation and alienation persists. Sitting in a tramcar, Roquentin is overcome by the brute existence of the seat oppposite him:

> I murmur: 'It's a seat', rather like an exorcism. But the word remains on my lips, it refuses to settle on the thing . . . Things have broken free from their names. They are there,

grotesque, stubborn, gigantic, and it seems ridiculous to call them seats or say anything at all about them.[9]

Roquentin's anguish culminates in an overwhelming experience when, whilst sitting in the park, his consciousness is invaded by the wordless and pressing existence of the roots of a chestnut tree. Thinking about this afterwards he realizes that we do not normally confront actual existence. We deal usually in appearances, classifying things by means of words, giving them significance through the uses we make of them. We rarely experience their meaningless and terrifying bulk presence. But in the park Roquentin realizes that to exist at all one must exist as things and objects exist; there is, he says, 'no half-way house between non-existence and this rapturous abundance'.[10]

Throughout the account of Roquentin's experiences in the park, the tramcar, and on the beach, Sartre is trying to describe what he calls the contingency or absurdity of existence. Roquentin can find no reason that explains the brute existence of things. He reflects that if one tried to define 'existence' the essential thing one would have to say is that it means that something just happens to be there: there is nothing that precedes existence which is a reason for existence and so gives it meaning. Contingency is bedrock. It so happens that things are there, and that is all there is to it. When, later, Roquentin writes about his experience in the park he says: 'The word Absurdity is now born beneath my pen . . . I, a little while ago, experienced the absolute, the absolute or the absurd'.[11] The absurdity he has recognized is the absurdity of contingency: the inexplicable existence of each and every thing, the ridiculousness of the world's being there. Sartre's descriptions of these episodes show us something of the difference between his concept of absurdity and that of Camus. Sartre described the difference in the following way:

Camus's philosophy is a philosophy of the absurd. For him the absurd arises from the relation between man and the world, between man's rational demands and the world's irrationality . . . What I call the absurd is something very different: the absurdity is the given, unjustifiable, primordial quality of existence.[12]

Sartre maintains that consciousness desires to exist with the fullness of being of an existing thing, but without any loss of consciousness or meaning. However, the desired embodying is never possible. Consciousness can never become an embodied thing *and* remain consciousness. The two regions of being are entirely distinct and the ideal of fusing them is what Sartre calls 'an unrealizable totality which haunts the For-itself and constitutes its very being as the nothingness of being'. And he says:

> It is this ideal which can be called God. Thus the best way to conceive of the fundamental project of human-reality is to say that man is the being whose project is to be God . . . To be man means to reach towards being God. Or if you prefer, man fundamentally is the desire to be God.[13]

This, of course, is 'what it is like' to be a human being. One can recognize, I think, in the desire of the For-itself to become embodied in an In-itself, the vague but permanent sense that most of us have of a quest for a personal existence that is both fully real and fully conscious of its reality.

4   MORALITY AND EXISTENTIAL SUICIDE

Mathieu's projected suicide exemplifies the existential point of view about self-killing. He does not think about it in relation to its effect on other people or to any duties or responsibilities he might be deemed to have. His central concern is to explore and risk the freedom which he now sees as the meaning of his own and all other human existence. He realizes, moreover, that this freedom is a total freedom. It is not that he merely has scope to choose between this or that moral or religious code, nor even that he finds, in his experience of his human-reality, some fundamental or intrinsic human values to which he can, if he so chooses, hold fast for guidance. What he perceives is a meaningless, gratuitous mass of existing things which, because they wholly lack any given or intrinsic values, can be given meaning only by the way in which he chooses to understand and deploy them. He may choose what value or meaning to place on what is present to his consciousness. He can change the meaning even of his past by the choice he makes in relation to it. Of course, the act of suicide at once abolishes the possibility of any further meanings since it abolishes the consciousness which is the source of meanings. Thus Sartre describes suicide as 'an absurdity which causes my life to be submerged in the absurd'.[14] Death, he says, is never that which gives life its meanings and death by suicide is not more meaningful than a natural death. What the act of suicide means is that '. . . in attempting to get rid of my life I affirm that I live and I assume this life as bad'. And he points out that 'to be dead is to be prey for the living'.[15] My death turns me into an object for other people, so that I can have only the meanings they give me. Death ends my subjectivity but it leaves my 'exterior' in the hands of others. He continues:

> So long as I live I can escape what I *am* for the Other by revealing to myself by my freely posited ends that I *am* nothing and that I make myself be what I am; so long as I live, I can give the lie to what others discover in me . . . Thus ceaselessly I escape my outside and ceaselessly I am reapprehended by the Other . . . But the *fact of death* . . . gives the final victory to the point of view of the Other . . . to die is to exist only through the Other, and to owe him one's meaning . . .[16]

Mathieu's thought that if he did kill himself his suicide would be 'an absolute, a law, a choice and a morality' reminds us that what counts from an existentialist point of view is the recognition, in the face of total freedom, of one's responsibility for all one's actions and the development of that recognition into an authentic choice. Thus to reject suicide on the grounds that it might cause more unhappiness than happiness, or is contrary to a particular set of beliefs would be, for the existentialist, more reprehensible than authentically choosing it. Morality is 'a personal structure of human reality'[17] and a freely-chosen suicide is a choice of oneself as 'a suicide': 'suicide, in fact, is a choice and affirmation – of being'.[18] The emphasis is entirely on the individual person as the source of values and meanings. This shows very vividly how far apart existentialism stands from more socially-oriented views of suicide. From a societal standpoint suicide is often diagnosed as the action of someone who has become utterly estranged or dislocated from the ordinary processes of life within a society, a community, or a family. There is a fairly widespread general belief that a great many suicides would not have occurred if only the persons concerned had been able to maintain just one or two significant personal relationships that would have preserved meaning for their lives. Existentialism contrasts sharply with this. In the first place, it does not regard a sense of alienation or dislocation as pathological or to be avoided, but rather as a prerequisite for realizing what free human existence is like. In the second place, and again this is especially clear in Sartre's thought, it often maintains that a profound union with another person, so often seen as a saving factor in cases of contemplated suicide, is as impossible as the union of a For-itself with an In-itself. In close personal relationships we long for a complete unity which yet preserves our separate awareness *of* that unity, just as we long to exist with the incorrigible reality of a solid object and yet retain a full consciousness of that reality. But these conditions, Sartre maintains, are never realizable. A sense of alienation and apartness is not simply something that may bring a person to the point of suicide, but a way of recognizing what it actually and inescapably is like to be a human being, and a necessary part of everyone's experience.

Another sharp contrast between an existentialist view of suicide and socially-oriented views shows up when we consider the nature of existential choice. What is important in existentialism is that the choice of action is also a choice of oneself in that one chooses, through one's actions, the way one will exist in the world. Thus, if I choose to kill myself, what is significant is that I have chosen to be a suicide, to exist as 'the person who killed herself'. This is seen as a choice of one's essence. We cannot choose our existence, for existence is 'given' in the sense that we just do find ourselves existing; but we may choose our essence, that is, our particular *ways* of existing in the world, and this is the meaning of a famous slogan of existentialism: 'Existence commands and precedes essence'.[19] Freedom is therefore the freedom to choose the meaning of one's existence.

According to Sartre, no thing, neither oneself as an In-itself nor any thing that exists can determine one's action. When I 'stand back' and become conscious of myself as a certain sort of person, the historical entity that I make of myself in standing back is not what decides my next action. Nor is the action or project that I envisage for myself a *thing*. It is the conjecture of a future possibility that does not yet exist. So although I may be conscious of myself as lonely or helpless or sick of life, and may consider suicide as a future possibility, it is not my despair that determines my choice of action, for the very awareness of what I now am provides the condition for recognizing the possibility of *not* existing in that way, of not despairing. In the moment of apprehension of what one is, one is no longer simply that In-itself but also a For-itself which is a no-thing. The choice of oneself is not made, and cannot be made, within the density of the In-itself where there is no room for the nothingness that makes choice possible. In becoming conscious of my condition I separate myself from it and am able to give it a meaning. I can see myself as someone who will shake off or confront my wretchedness and find a new life project; or as someone who moves towards self-destruction, or who is indecisive; or I can see myself in numerous other ways. Sartre describes this choice of oneself as being dependent on a kind of double nothingness: I have to think of my present state as nothing in order to recognize the possibility of changing it, and I have to think of my future as nothing, in order to choose my way of existing in it.

Still one wants to ask: What, nevertheless, makes me choose the way of being in the world that I do choose? What, for example, if I am contemplating suicide, makes me opt for continuing with my life rather than killing myself? Surely choice must be determined in some way? In the face of such questioning, Sartre simply reaffirms that there is no given set of values that we discover or learn and in accordance with which we have to determine our ends or purposes. Nor have we, he says, a given essential nature which shapes choices: existence is prior to essence and I have no essence until I give myself one in choosing myself. And so our choice is absurd, because it is made on the basis of nothing. There are no reasons for choosing as we do choose, but we have to make a choice of some sort. It is as if, in the upsurge of consciousness, we encounter ourselves as beings and this very encountering bestows a value and meaning on what is encountered. The way in which we become conscious of ourselves is a choice or defining of ourselves. But it is ungrounded because it is made out of nothingness. Sartre calls this choice 'the radical decision'.

5   'THE RADICAL DECISION'

Sartre's analysis of 'the radical decision' is worth close attention. He is acutely critical of the kind of psychological analysis that is often given as an explanation of human personality. He considers the writer Flaubert, whose biographers had described him as 'ambitious' and had then explained this characteristic as being the result of inherited traits, learned behaviour patterns and environmental influences. Sartre rejects this account because it has treated Flaubert as if he were like a chemical substance, analysable in terms of properties and molecules, and thus not responsible for what he essentially is. In contrast, Sartre wants to maintain that neither Flaubert nor any other person merely 'receives' their essence. He says:

> Neither heredity nor bourgeois background nor education can account for it . . . In one sense Flaubert's ambition is a fact with all a fact's contingency . . . but in another sense *it makes itself*, and . . . we may be able to grasp beyond this ambition something more, something like a radical decision which, without ceasing to be contingent, would be the veritable psychic irreducible.[20]

In saying that Flaubert's ambition is 'a fact with all a fact's contingency', what Sartre is insisting on is that to be ambitious is a choice, made by Flaubert, on the basis of nothing. It is Flaubert's 'radical decision' concerning his way of being in the world. His choice is therefore free and meaningful rather than the inevitable product of inherited tendencies, upbringing and environment. The ambition 'makes itself' in that nothing else produces it. Flaubert has chosen to be in the world 'ambitiously' and the choice is irreducible because, since nothing determines it, there is no further explanation or reason for its being what it is. A human being is not to be regarded as a substance-with-properties but as what Sartre calls 'a non-substantial absolute'; a person is 'a psychic irreducible' rather than a neutral substance that is passively receptive to impressions. He points out that a causal investigation cannot provide a conclusive explanation of someone's being ambitious or self-effacing or suicidal or, indeed, anything else. We have therefore to resist seeking explanations that try to go further and further beyond or beneath what is open to view. Here Sartre is contending against all psychoanalytic theory as well as determinism in general. His own method, which he calls existential psychoanalysis, seeks to comprehend a person's fundamental choice. It regards a person as 'a mystery in broad daylight', a totality and not a mere collection of properties; someone who is to be understood rather than conceptualized. For any attempt to conceptualize the fundamental choice must fail, and the type of understanding of a person that is possible cannot strictly be described as 'knowledge'. It is more a recognition that someone exists in just the way she does and in no other way, and of there being no ultimate reason for her being as she is other than that she has chosen herself in that way. The implications of this analysis of the human person are that each one of us, whether suicidal, ambitious, or anything else, is responsible for the way in which we value, define, and deploy our existences. Even if someone rejected the responsibility the existential view of that rejection would be that the person had freely chosen himself or herself as someone who refused responsibility, since freedom itself, however much we try to turn away from it, is inescapable. It is the human condition. Thus, for the existentialist confronted with the innumerable choices of life, it is not so much what one chooses as the manner of choice that is important. At every moment I have to make myself; that is, I have to exist in *some* way as some particular being. If I recognize and acknowledge that the choice of what I will be is made on the basis of nothing, then I understand my responsibility for myself. I recognize what Sartre calls my 'gratuitousness' and the ultimate contingency of everything. I see that I just happen to exist and that there is no laid-down meaning or purpose that is given along with existence.

6 'BAD FAITH' AND ANGUISH

The recognition of ultimate pointlessness, of contingency, produces existential anguish. Roquentin experiences anguish as the result of the 'nausea' he feels in the presence of the chestnut trees in the park and when looking at the seat in the tramcar. He is terrified by the thought that only he can inaugurate or abolish his values and meanings and that this is what human reality consists of. At the same time, he despises those who, in their anguish, try to turn away from the burden of being responsible for themselves; those who, in Sartre's term, act in 'bad faith'. Bad faith is the evasion of existential anguish. It has many forms. One manifestation of it occurs in the person who opts for a rôle or lifestyle that is a mere stereotype or cliché. Overwhelmed by the responsibility of choosing a meaning and a value for his life, a person may find a partial escape and a superficial consolation in adopting a ready-made rôle which provides him with a meaning he does not have to make for himself. Instead of living as a subject who is fully aware of his freedom and assumes responsibility for himself, he treats himself as a thing or object that has a designated function to fulfil. Sartre's most famous example concerns a waiter:

> Let us consider this waiter in the café. His movement is quick and forward, a little too precise, a little too rapid. He comes towards the patrons with a step a little too quick . . . his voice, his eyes express an interest a little too solicitous for the order of the customer . . . he gives himself the quickness and pitiless rapidity of things . . . the waiter in the cafe plays with his condition in order to realize it.[21]

Sartre tries to image himself as a waiter and ponders on the impossibility of actually embodying his consciousness in a rôle so that he becomes a thing. He says: 'I cannot be he [a waiter], I can only play at *being* him; that is, imagine to myself that I am he'.[22] It is as if he finds that some inward aspect of himself, whatever he does in his endeavour to exist 'as a waiter', simply is *not* that waiter; indeed, is no-thing or object, but rather a consciousness *of* things. He maintains that even those who seem to feel they have succeeded in making themselves into something such as a doctor, a student, a socialite, an intellectual, a waiter and so on, are living in bad faith; for in adopting the stereotyped characteristics of those rôles they are deceiving themselves.

The idea of deceiving oneself is somewhat complicated. In order to deceive at all, one must know the truth of a matter. Otherwise what one does is not a deception but an error, or something done in ignorance. Bad faith is a form of lying to oneself, but it is difficult to see how one can both confront a truth and deceive oneself about it. Yet this does seem to be something that people commonly engage in: an ignoring of something recognized as a truth, and a holding fast to an illusion. At the same time, bad faith is a *faith*. In it, we manage to establish a belief in ideas which we have set up simply in order to persuade ourselves that something is other than it is, or that we are what we are not. A man who runs a business, for example, may hold to a false faith in himself as a fair and sympathetic employer and ignore the fact that all he does is actually to further his own profit. He refuses to see himself as he actually is, and sets himself up as what he is not, shunning the evidence in his deeds that would remind him of the truth about himself. But his whole being, on an existential analysis, is in disintegration because any kind of choice he makes of himself is made in relation not to what he actually is but to what he is not. His choice is made in relation to a lie he has told himself about himself.

The concept of bad faith relates interestingly to certain aspects of the psychology of suicide. Attempts to commit suicide quite frequently fail and it is often thought that many such attempts are intended to fail: they are described as 'cries for help' rather than whole-hearted endeavours to end life. It is this kind of case that can sometimes be understood more fully through a consideration of bad faith. We can easily imagine a woman, say, who has been rejected in a love relationship and who feels abandoned, insulted, lonely and angry. But instead of seeing her unhappiness in quite those terms she casts herself in the rôle of the inconsolable and star-crossed lover. Her pain and anger feed on this image and she comes to see herself as 'the woman who wishes to be dead because her love is unrequited' rather than someone who is hurt and angered by rejection. Her attempt at suicide is then a choice made in accordance with her false view of what she is, and the failure of the suicide attempt is a manifestation of that vestige of genuine knowledge of her anger and of her real desire to make her former lover feel guilty and repent his rejection of her. A successful suicide could not satisfy her real aim, for then she would not have the satisfaction of witnessing the stir her death would occasion and the guilt and remorse of the man who had abandoned her. This is not to say that all failed suicides are to be understood in this way but that some may be, once the protagonists have been able to examine and reflect on what they have done. Nor is to suggest that all successful suicides are, simply in virtue of being successful, cases of authentic and free choice. For something that was meant simply as a gesture might, by chance or bad management, end in death; and something meant to be inescapably final might, in like manner, fail to bring about the end of everything.

Closely connected with bad faith is what Sartre calls 'the spirit of seriousness'. This 'seriousness' has two characteristics. The first is that it takes values to exist quite independently of human beings, as somehow given to us. The second is that it takes those values to be materially embodied in things. Thus it might take 'nourishment' to be part of the actual material of bread. Serious-mindedness can affect all kinds of judgements, not just moral ones. In the presence of works of art, for instance, if I am serious-minded, I will search assiduously for values embodied in the works and so will not exercise my freedom to make my own judgements. In not confronting my freedom to choose values I evade or avoid the anguish of realizing my responsibility for my deeds and my judgements. For if I believe that things already contain their values then I am saved the anguish of choosing values for them and admitting my responsibility for that choice. For such a person, Sartre says, 'Objects are mute demands, and he is nothing in himself but the passive obedience to those demands'.[23] In reflecting about suicide, if I am Sartre's serious-minded person then I may see suicide as bearing its own value; as being, perhaps, something that is intrinsically cowardly and wrong whatever its circumstances. And if I see *that* as the value and meaning of suicide then, if I choose it as my course of action, the meaning it gives to me is that I have behaved in a wrong and cowardly way. I have not freely made a meaning for myself; I have merely conformed to one which I have taken to exist independently of me.

The anguish experienced in the realization of one's freedom should not be underestimated. Sartre says: 'It is certain that we cannot overcome anguish for we *are* anguish'.[24] However, we do try to evade it in many ways, often by positing a determinism through which we think of ourselves as objects driven by forces other than ourselves and therefore not obliged to choose what we shall be and not responsible for what we are. But Sartre points out that in order to evade something I must know what it is: 'I must think of it constantly in order to take care not to think of it'.[25] When we stand by a precipice or on a height and experience a feeling of vertigo this, he suggests, is an experience of anguish. It is different from fear in that fear is of objects external to oneself whereas 'anguish is anguish before myself' and is not evoked by things. Vertigo is a manifestation of anguish insofar as 'I am afraid not of falling over the precipice but of throwing myself over'. It relates to what I might possibly do rather than to what might happen to me. It is possible that I might choose, in the next moment, something appalling and terrible such as impulsively ending my life, for when nothing determines one's choice there is the possibility of choosing anything at all, simply because the choice is made for no reason. Sartre gives the example of negotiating a path that runs along the edge of a precipice. In spite of all the care taken in such a situation, the foresight and calculation of the difficulties and one's cautious and controlled movements, there is still the possibility not simply of the occurrence of mishap or accident, but of one's choosing to be reckless or wild, of choosing suddenly to jump over the edge. Although there may be nothing conducive to doing this, although there is no reason for such a choice, although its prospect is horrifying, yet *one might just choose to kill oneself.* He says:

> I am in anguish precisely because any conduct on my part is only possible, and this means that while constituting a totality of motives for pushing away that situation, I at the same moment apprehend these motives as not sufficiently effective. At the very moment when I apprehend my being as horror of the precipice, I am conscious of that horror as not determinant in relation to my possible conduct. In one sense that horror calls for prudent conduct, and it is in itself a pre-outline of that conduct; in another sense, it posits the final developments of that conduct only as possible, precisely because I do not apprehend it as the cause of these final developments . . .[26]

7   GOOD FAITH

What exactly would it be like to choose suicide in *good* faith? Sartre gives no positive account of good faith and we have, in the main, to formulate an idea of it by construing it as an opposition to or countering of bad faith. Bad faith is a division or disintegration of one's being, a move to become an In-itself to which one gives a false name, as in the case of the woman who thinks of herself as ready to kill herself for unrequited love rather than as angry and vindictive. Good faith must then seek to prevent this self-deception and restore an integrity between one's choice and one's action. It is a denial of a denial. The first denial is when, in bad faith, the woman denies her anger and vindictiveness; the second denial is good faith's denial of that self-deception. Suicide performed in good faith must therefore consist of a certain kind of coherence between one's choice of oneself and the action that fulfils, or attempts to fulfil, the choice. Good faith begins to look like a form of sincerity. But now, perhaps, difficulties begin to show. The person who looks me in the eye, declaring his complete sincerity, is surely a prime example of *bad* faith. For he has cast himself, and now presents himself, in the role of 'a completely sincere person' and this reflective presentation has somehow poisoned what might have been a spontaneous sincerity. Sartre speaks of the pupil who wishes to be attentive, his eyes riveted on the teacher, his ears open wide, but who 'so exhausts himself in playing the attentive role that he ends up by no longer hearing anything'.[27] We are face-to-face again with the futile longing to exist with all the fullness of a thing but without loss of awareness. Sartre says:

> In introspection I try . . . to make up my mind to be my true self without delay – even though it means consequently to set about searching for ways to change myself. But what does this mean if not that I am constituting myself as a thing? . . . what then is sincerity except precisely a phenomenon of bad faith?[28]

Good faith, it seems, must consist in speaking and acting truly without noting *that* one is doing so. It is believing something without the thought *that* one believes. It requires this immediacy in order not to be bad faith, and yet the very requirement strips away that dimension of self-consciousness that makes human reality what it is and that is the condition of freedom and choice. Sartre in fact maintains that good faith is never entirely achievable and that bad faith is to some extent unavoidable however much we desire to live in good faith. He once described human life as 'a useless passion'. The passion is to be God; but it is a useless passion because it is impossible for a human being to become God. The ideal of complete good faith is nothing strange or new. It coincides with and is perhaps just another expression of our common understanding of the truly virtuous person. We sense that the goodness of such a person is somehow unpremeditated and spontaneous. He sees the good and is drawn irresistibly to it. There is no alternative, for he is not *conscious* of any alternative. He seems in some sense not to be responsible for his virtue because he is not conscious of it as virtue.

If a suicide can be committed in good faith then it must surely be one in which the overriding wish and purpose of the person concerned is to end his life. Sometimes the close friends and relatives of a suicide speak of the inevitability with which the suicide, over a period of time, seemed to move towards the commission of the act. They recognize its ultimate unpreventability. The suicide himself sees no alternative, and no real alternative comes to mind. His death may be terrible, but it is not terrible to him in the way it is to those who would want to prevent it. As with Mathieu's contemplated drowning by leaping from the parapet of the Pont-Neuf, his suicide is 'an absolute, a law, a choice, and a morality'.

8   THE SARTREAN POINT OF VIEW

One reason why Sartre deals so scantily with the notions of good faith and authenticity in *Being and Nothingness* is that the purpose of his enquiry there is to provide a description of the structures of human life rather than a prescription for living it. Thus he is not purporting to offer advice on what people ought to do but an analysis of the kind of beings they are; nor does he say that people ought to make free choices, but that human existence is such that they cannot avoid making choices and that a choice made in bad faith is as much a choice as is a choice made in good faith. We should not therefore think of *Being and Nothingness* as thinly-disguised moral exhortation. However, the terms 'bad faith' and 'good faith' contain their own judgements of demerit and merit respectively and it is clear that existentialism values good faith and authenticity and averts from bad faith and 'seriousness'. We are, moreover, acutely aware of the deep moral concern that informs all Sartre's writing, including works such as *Being and Nothingness* that are purportedly to do with the nature of being rather than ethics. But then, moral concern and the concerns of morality are surely inescapable in any enquiry into the experience of being a human being. István Mészáros has remarked of Sartre's moral philosophy that it is 'not an explicit but a latent moral philosophy . . . he cannot write it because he does write it – in a diffuse form – all the time'.[29] In saying this he is pointing out that in order to do his kind of philosophy Sartre has to live his moral sensibility, moving onwards all the time to think and write in the space between what he was a moment ago and what he will become in the next moment. For him, to write an explicit moral philosophy would be to capitulate to seriousness and bad faith since it would involve formulating precepts, rules, even a system, that would nullify the conditions under which moral conduct is possible. But in writing in just the way he does write, Sartre is engaging in moral philosophy.

Perhaps one of the greatest merits of existentialism is that, in ethical as in other matters, it invites and provides the conditions for consideration of particular individuals and particular cases. True, such considerations have to be made in relation to what turns out to be a somewhat vague concept of authenticity. But even this vagueness preserves and reinforces certain important characteristics of morality, namely, the ultimate openness and uncertainty of its judgements, and the requirement to commit oneself to a view or an attitude based in the last resort on a personal conviction. Nowhere are such characteristics more clearly revealed than in judgements and reflections concerning suicide. But it is arguable, too, that this great merit of existentialism, its emphasis on the individual, is also a demerit, for most of our decisions and actions occur in the context of and have direct relevance to our relationships with other people and it is, on the whole, those relationships rather than the extremes of individualism that form the enduring and significant core of a person's moral sensibility.

Because existentialism is a philosophy of personal existence, the best way to understand it and equip oneself to assess it is imaginatively to inhabit it for a while; to try it on, so to speak, to see if it fits one's own existence. Sartre's careful descriptions are important elements in his argument; for if a description of something is so apt and precise that we cannot fail to agree that this is 'what it is like', then we have made the first move towards acceptance of the broader account of 'what it is like to exist as a human being'. He illuminates for us the nature of a personal existence in which we view ourselves as a subject as well as an object. He describes reality as it were from the receiving end, from the point of view of the participant in it, and not as an observer might describe it in terms of interactions between one object, the human being, and another object, the world. He forces us to climb back inside the skin of our own experience and develop an awareness of the most general and essential structure of personal existence. Nevertheless, reading Sartre can be difficult if one happens to be of a temperament very different from his. For although his whole purpose is to give an account of the most general features of human existence, a large part of this method consists in giving particular examples of them; and so it may well be that, in spite of the generality of a feature to be illustrated, we may fail to recognize it as such because we fail to respond to the particular example of it. Lacking common ground for a shared experience, we may then reject the whole account without further consideration. A case of this is Roquentin's strange malady. For him, the physical existence and multi-plicity of things is experienced as an overwhelming nausea or sickness. He is engulfed by a terror of the cloying invasion of meaningless, coagulate matter that might flow into every corner of his being. For others, however, although they may from time to time be overwhelmed by the experience of the bulk presence and the senseless, spreading fecundity of existence, the term 'nausea' will not do, even though they may share Roquentin's anguish. But this is where Sartre's attention to detail and his literary art can help. Somewhere in the description of the minutiae of Roquentin's experience, we may be able to recognize an emotion or a response that is also our own. The more one reads, the more one is able to connect one's own experiences with his, tying them in thread by thread with each other. In this way one may be able to come to see one's own experience as fundamentally similar in many respects to Roquentin's.

Something that has to be questioned in Sartre is his characterization of the relationship between consciousness and things. For him, this relationship seems to be fundamentally one of conflict or struggle but it is by no means obvious that the whole story of the relationship can be told in terms of the desperate circumventing by consciousness of a relentless invasion of what Sartre sometimes calls the 'viscosity' of the In-itself, the incorrigible density of things. Most of his examples, especially in *Nausea*, carry strong implications of a necessary evil in the relationship. Yet we can, if we wish, cite equally vivid but quite different sorts of examples in it. For our consciousness of the teeming and multitudinous presence of things may well engender delight *that* the world is there in all its abundance and profusion. And there can obtain, between consciousness and things, a relationship in which we value things for their own sakes, exercising a sensuous care for objects and for the physicality of the world. In such a relationship delight of the senses is seen as a proper pleasure. In a similar way, Sartre's lengthy descriptions of the anguish which he maintains is the very structure of our realization of our total and groundless freedom can lead us to forget that anguish need not be the enduring consequence of that realization. For a sense of total freedom, although realized in anguish, may well generate exhilaration and adventurousness, liberating one from a restless search for meaning *in* things. The existential viewpoint should not therefore be seen as consisting solely of despair in the face of absurdity. Sartre himself, in defending his ideas against imputations of pessimism, has said that it cannot be regarded so, 'for no doctrine is more optimistic – the destiny of man is placed within himself'.[30] His analysis of human-reality establishes formal conditions that provide as much scope for affirming life as for denying it and it is important to remember this when one is confronted with some of the extreme and highly charged situations Sartre uses to make his ideas vivid.

What has existentialism to say to the charge sometimes made against it that it is too much concerned with the self? I think the response might be to point out that anyone making that charge has misunderstood Sartre's enterprise. For Sartre, as has already been mentioned, is primarily offering an account of the way things are rather than a prescription for living one's life, and if his account of human-reality is correct then the centrality of the self – in some sense of the term 'self' – follows from that account. He says: 'Human reality exists for the purpose of itself – and it's that *self*, with its specific type of existence . . . which is value'.[31] Underlying this claim is Sartre's analysis of human reality as a consciousness that is aware, first, of not being the foundation of its own being and, second, of being responsible for itself. Because we do not found ourselves, that is, do not determine our presence in the world but simply discover ourselves existing, we are, Sartre says, 'gratuitous'. But we are also, in virtue of the very structure of our consciousness, morally aware that we are responsible for ourselves. Our presence in the world is gratuitous and has no foundation, but consciousness, the For-itself, assumes the task of making its own foundation for itself. It does this by its projects: that is, by engaging in actions that will give its presence meaning and value. Thus, a project of mine may be to become a teacher of philosophy and thereby to make a meaning for myself that will be my foundation in the future. Sartre held that any such foundation is an illusion but that the human urge to be one's own foundation is a moral one. In the *War Diaries* he wrote:

> Human reality is moral because it wishes to be its own foundation . . . Man is a being who flees from himself into the future. Throughout all his undertakings he seeks, not to preserve himself, as people have often said, nor to increase himself, but to found himself. And at the end of each undertaking he finds himself anew just as he was: gratuitous to the marrow.[32]

The special situation of human reality is that it is not its own cause, that is, it is not self-originating; yet it necessarily is self-motivating and wholly responsible for what it makes of itself. In short, one does not choose one's existence but one is nevertheless responsible for it. The structure of consciousness is such that it throws itself 'forwards into the world to escape this gratuitousness'[33] in order to be its own foundation in the future. It envisages what it might become, and this is its project; but when the envisaged project is brought about, even if it is exactly as envisaged, still consciousness is not and cannot be its own foundation. This is because the project itself is not consciousness, and when it is realized, when 'this future becomes present', consciousness will be still simply consciousness: a nothingness that is not the realized project it is conscious *of*, and which once again has to motivate itself out of nothingness rather than from the realized project. This is why Sartre says that at the end of each undertaking a person 'finds himself anew just as he was: gratuitous to the marrow'. Awareness of death belongs with our awareness of gratuitousness, of not being the cause of oneself. Sartre says that death is recognized as a possibility but cannot be comprehended as a possibility for consciousness. This is because consciousness cannot conceive of its own death, since that would involve being conscious of death and would therefore involve the existence of what one is trying to conceive of as dead. He says: 'every consciousness is numbed by Nothingness and by death, without even being able to turn on this Nothingness and look it in the face.'[34]

One cannot become conscious of one's death but consciousness of the acts that constitute one's suicide is perfectly possible. Suicide can be a project for consciousness and there does not seem to be any reason within existentialism why it cannot be undertaken in good faith. Sartre makes it clear that a suicide committed in bad faith is as much a choice as one committed in good faith and that no one is therefore 'driven to suicide'. It is always chosen. Concerning those extreme situations that evoke feelings of total despair he writes:

The point is not to say, with the saint: 'It's too much, O Lord, it's too much'. Nothing is ever too much. For – at the very moment when I lose my grip, when my body 'overcomes me', when under physical torment I confess what I wanted to keep secret – it is of my own accord, through the free consciousness of my torment, that I decide to confess . . .[35]

It is the same with suicide:

it is always upon me that the terrible responsibility falls of acknowledging that I am defeated; and, at whatever point I stop, it is I who have decided I couldn't go on any longer – hence I could have gone on a bit longer still. But I admit – and wish – never to have any excuse, my freedom becomes mine, I assume for ever that terrible responsibility.[36]

NOTES

1 Sartre, J.-P. (1963) *The Reprieve*, Penguin, pp. 308–9.
2 Sartre, J.-P. (1953) *Being and Nothingness*, Hazel E. Barnes (trans.), Methuen.
3 Sartre (1963), *op. cit.*, p. 309.
4 Sartre (1953), *op cit.*, pp. xliii and 74.
5 *Ibid.*, p. xliii.
6 *Ibid.*, p. 25.
7 Sartre, J.-P. (1965) *Nausea*, Penguin.
8 *Ibid.*, p. 22.
9 *Ibid.*, p. 180.
10 *Ibid.*, p. 183.
11 *Ibid.*, p. 185.
12 Sartre, J.-P. (1945) *Paru*, December.
13 Sartre (1953), *op. cit.*, p. 566.
14 *Ibid.*, p. 540.
15 *Ibid.*, p. 543.
16 *Ibid.*, p. 544.
17 Sartre, J.-P. (1985) *War Diaries*, Quentin Hoare (trans.), Verso, p. 108.
18 Sartre (1953), *op. cit.*, p. 479.
19 *Ibid.*, p. 438.
20 *Ibid.*, p. 560.
21 *Ibid.*, p. 59.
22 *Ibid.*, p. 60.
23 *Ibid.*, p. 626.
24 *Ibid.*, p. 43.
25 *Ibid.*
26 *Ibid.*, p. 31.

27 *Ibid.*, p. 60.
28 *Ibid.*, p. 63.
29 Mészáros, István (1979) *The Philosophy of Sartre*, vol. I, Harvester, p. 61.
30 Sartre, J.-P. (1973) *Existentialism and Humanism*, Philip Mairet (trans.), Methuen, p. 44.
31 Sartre (1985), *op. cit.*, p. 108.
32 *Ibid.*, p. 110.
33 *Ibid.*
34 *Ibid.*
35 *Ibid.*, p. 113.
36 *Ibid.*, p. 114.

CHAPTER FIVE

Morality and suicide

1 EXISTENTIALISM CONSIDERED

Sartre's view has to be seen as a part of the development of this book's discussion of attitudes towards suicide.

At one time moral approval or disapproval of suicide, as of other actions, was heavily influenced by religious thought. In general self-killing was judged to be both sinful and criminal because it flouted God's law. There were.exceptions to this dominant attitude and there were those who were ready to argue that certain forms of suicide were enactments rather than floutings of that authority. Donne's *Biathanatos* is an example of a sustained attempt to argue that suicide was not always and necessarily a contravention of holy law. But Donne did not try to alter the theological structure from which the dominant attitude was formed. His aim was to show what kinds of views about suicide might be legitimately derived from it. A noteworthy feature of his approach is that he recognized, perhaps largely in virtue of his own passionate and inward disposition, the variety and strength of individual feelings and tendencies. And he saw that suicide, because it is both self-directed and self-assertive, is to do with the relationship of a person's inward self to God, or the unknown, and to life.

By the end of the eighteenth century a more secular morality, represented in this book by the views of David Hume, had taken hold. On this kind of view God was thought of as the creator of all things and as having established a law-governed natural order as a framework within which human beings could pursue their personal and social well-being by devising 'artificial' laws that were founded on the natural ones. From this basis the view was developed that the morality of suicide was a social rather than a religious concern and that its rightness or wrongness was to be judged by reference to its effect on the general well-being. Suicide became, at an intellectual level, the object of rational consideration and tolerance, and there is a good deal in this attitude that is reminiscent of the pre-Christian attitudes of Greece and Rome in which a concern for one's personal honour and dignity, as well as for civic and social obligations, were taken into account in considering suicide. At an emotional level, the general and spontaneous response in the eighteenth century to most cases of self-killing continued to be one of shock and regret. Wanting to prevent suicide was, and still is, a first natural reaction to the threat of it.

The nineteenth-century utilitarianism that developed from Hume's moral philosophy was not adequate for reflecting on or resolving many of the issues connected with suicide. Its chief concern was with increasing the quantities of general happiness and it therefore gave little weight to the personal and inward aspects of self-killing. Moreover, its severance of morality from any essential connection with a religious foundation meant that it was unable to respond to thoughts, so often invoked by reflections on suicide, about meanings and values lying beyond the immediacy of the aspects of life to which the happiness principle is applied. Such thoughts are given a setting when we turn to philosophers such as Schopenhauer, who wanted to find an underlying reality that unified experience; to Camus, who confronts the intuition that there is no ultimate meaning to life; and to Sartre, who develops a detailed account of the human being as wholly free and as responsible for the making of all his or her choices and values.

The dimensions of the personal and the metaphysical that are largely neglected by utilitarian moralities are well-established in Sartrean existentialism and it does seem in many respects to offer an appropriate context in which to deliberate about suicide. It emphasizes autonomy and personal responsibility, demands rigorous self-examination and a questioning of accepted rules or codes of behaviour, and conducts its enquiry within the context of an account of the fundamental features of human existence. True, it can be dismaying to think that the fact of the existence of everything is to be seen as a merely contingent fact and yet, absurdly, the ground of everything. But it is just that conception that provides the conditions of the complete human freedom for which Sartre argues. Beyond that first dismay the existentialist framework can make a person's sense of freedom, responsibility and autonomy more vivid.

However, it follows from Sartre's views on the groundlessness of choice that no guidance on specific courses of action can be derived from existentialism. The fundamental existential value is to 'found oneself' by willingly assuming responsibility for every aspect of oneself. A secondary value of existentialism is the exercise of authenticity in making the choices that constitute that founding and in committing oneself to the project one sets for oneself. But the moral efficacy of particular courses of action, problems of conflicts between duties and interests, and criteria for making one's choices have no place in a theory that has argued that human-reality is the freedom to make values out of nothing. Existentialism offers a formal structure, a blueprint for a manner of existing at a high level of generality, but nothing that helps one to see what in particular one might be or do in order to live and die well. At the end of *Being and Nothingness* Sartre remarks that although much of his discussion is 'on the moral plane'[1] it has dealt mainly with the morality produced by bad faith, 'an ethic which is ashamed of itself'. What he has wanted to show, he says, is that the moral agent is 'the being by whom values exist'[2] and he reserves discussion of an ethics based on that understanding to a future work. That work was never written but Sartre leaves us with a question that he thought would be central to it: whether the supreme value might simply be the consciousness of the unrealizable 'aspiration to be God' or whether it might be something further, something that might transcend that very condition of perpetual aspiration.

Although existentialism may be judged unacceptable because of its particular metaphysical structure, or inadequate because it provides no content for morality, that does not mean that it must be totally rejected. It is possible to let go its metaphysical structure but to hold fast to and develop one or two of its themes and to give them a content that will provide substance for thoughts about suicide. What I want to hold fast to and develop are the following: first, the idea of assuming responsibility for oneself; and second, the thought that we do make our values and our moral selves, though not that we do so on the basis of nothing. Additionally, I shall suggest that what we do flows from what we are and from what we make of ourselves; that what is needed is much more particularity in thinking about and describing what we are and might be, since that is prior, and that this particularity requires reference to virtues and characteristics that are not chosen entirely on the basis of nothing but that are accepted or adopted, in part by reflection on an inherited and taught moral tradition, in part by the exercise of moral imagination. I want to say: we both discover *and* make our morality, and that what we discover and make is a conception of what it is to be a good person. In what follows I shall develop some thoughts about what it is to be a good person.

2 BEING AND DOING

The view that morality should be fundamentally concerned with what one ought to be rather than with what one ought to do is not new. Advocacy and criticism of it are part of the history of moral philosophy. The view does not dismiss questions of what to do as unimportant and it recognizes the point that what people do, especially what they do consistently and habitually, contributes vitally to what they become. But it tends to see morality as, in the first instance, a personal rather than a social matter and, as I have already suggested, it maintains that one's choice of an action will follow from what one is and that for this reason what one is is of first importance. In general, such a view rejects the existentialist idea of making a choice on the basis of nothing, though not the idea that one might come to change one's moral stance fundamentally or that it might be transformed or developed extensively. It places its emphasis on a person's character rather than on the rightness or wrongness of actions, and on reflection about what it is to be a good person. This reflection has, for much of its content, the moral tradition one finds oneself inhabiting and the moral commitments one has taken on or acquired as part of one's education and upbringing. The use of moral imagination to understand the inherited tradition and to resolve one's stance to the present and the future is an important part of this reflective activity, for almost any situation can be seen from several different moral points of view. One has to consider what possible moral descriptions might apply and then come to some view of one's own. This is why I suggest that we 'both discover and make our morality'. The 'making' need not produce any highly original moral innovation. The point is that it is a personal activity, not just in the existentialist sense that it is a choice of oneself, though I shall maintain that it does involve a certain making of self, but in that one is active in trying to perceive a situation as it actually, and perhaps complexly, is.

It is of course question-begging to speak of 'a situation as it actually is', but philosophers who favour the kind of view I have described broadly concur in speaking of perceiving, seeing, and attending to a matter or a person as being of the utmost importance in morality. John Kekes, in an article called 'Moral Sensitivity', writes: 'My claim is that one crucial moral task is to perceive accurately the situation in which one is called upon to act'.[3] This accurate perception, he argues, is not just of facts but concerns the significance of agreed-upon facts and he suggests that we use what he calls 'moral idioms' to determine this significance. Moral idioms, he says, describe character-traits and as examples he lists terms of moral approval and disapproval such as 'generous', 'faithful', 'courageous', 'forthright', 'envious', 'petty', 'cowardly' and 'arrogant'. Moral idioms are made available to us through our culture and our knowledge of other cultures and we recognize that the idioms have different significances in different cultures and at different times. What Kekes describes as 'moral sensitivity' depends on how a person is able to deploy moral idioms. Moral sensitivity can acquire breadth through realizing that conventional morality is simply the form of morality one happens to be born into. Kekes writes:

> To appreciate the endless variations possible on the theme provided by a moral idiom is to have a breadth of moral understanding. Courage may be physical bravery, the willingness to incur unpopularity, the quiet determination to continue as one has in a world gone mad, opposition to misguided authority, or risking one's well-being for a principle.[4]

There can be indecision and disagreement about what moral idiom to apply, as, for example, when a self-killing may be seen as cowardly in that it is an escape from something, courageous in that it is a bold step into the unknown. But Kekes remarks that:

> If I am satisfied by my characterisation of a situation in terms of a moral idiom, then what I ought to do is usually clear . . . Of course, problems remain. For knowing what I ought to do does not tell me how I ought to do it, and how much of it, or at what cost to myself I ought to do it. But moral idioms do guide us to the kind of action we should perform.[5]

A comparable attitude of seeing, perceiving or attending to something is described by Iris Murdoch in 'The Idea of Perfection'. Murdoch uses the word 'attention' to express, she says, 'the idea of a just and loving gaze directed upon an individual reality' and she regards this as 'the characteristic and proper mark of the active moral agent'.[6] She suggests that this activity goes on more or less continuously and that through it we build structures of values which are used when we make choices. Attending to something in this manner is a moral activity in a way that simply 'looking' at something is not. 'Looking' may be neutral or may produce false pictures and false understandings, but attention is what leads to what she describes as 'a refined and honest perception of what is really the case, a patient and just discernment and exploration of what confronts one'. Murdoch remarks that: 'If I attend properly I will have no choices and this is the ultimate condition to be aimed at'.[7] The remark echoes numerous other accounts of there being some sort of necessity connected with an accurate apprehension of what is morally good, in that something 'follows from' the experience of it. Wittgenstein mentions this when he talks of 'the absolutely right road'. He says, 'I think it would be a road which *everybody* on seeing it would, *with logical necessity*, have to go or be ashamed for not going'. Similarly, 'the absolute good', he says, would be a state of affairs 'which everybody, independent of his tastes and inclinations, would *necessarily* bring about or feel guilty for not bringing about'.[8] The same kind of necessity is expressed in the dictum 'Love God and do as you please'. That remark does not mean that anything goes as long as you love God but that *if* you love God you cannot go wrong insofar as you act out of that love; that loving God necessarily shows a person the perfect way.

3   A MORAL SELF

To be a person who directs 'a just and loving gaze' on the world and whose character and disposition are consonant with this attentive activity is to be someone who is conversant with and sensitive to the moral idioms of which Kekes writes: that whole range of virtues and vices that provides a context for recognizing moral possibilities and which is the rich resource we use in making judgements and moving towards actions. Kekes maintains that depth as well as breadth is required for moral sensitivity since breadth alone may produce only a confusing muddle of shifting values, 'that facile relativism many social scientists put in the way of moral understanding'.[9] Depth is what enables one to form a view for oneself about the possibilities that breadth has perceived and to realign one's picture of one's own moral being. It is a conscious process in which one's wants and commitments are considered, reviewed and related to one's ideals. Action is, of course, a product of this concern but choice of action is not its primary interest.

What Kekes describes as 'depth' seems to be the condition for making one's morality by forming a moral self; by becoming someone who has adopted and who continues to adopt specific virtues and values for oneself, placing some virtues above others, taking on some commitments in preference to others, aspiring to some ideals rather than others. This is not to suggest that in forming a moral self one reaches a settled position that puts an end to further reflection or precludes change and innovation; yet it may, for many, establish a foundation that does not alter radically in the course of time, whatever refinements and development it undergoes.

To develop a moral self it seems that one has gradually to form a personal realm that becomes a life that is within the wider life of the world and which is linked to the life of the world; it is to make a morality within morality in general. This does not mean that one has to think of the self as some kind of absolute or metaphysical entity, but rather as comprising the character of one's life as expressed thorough one's ideals and intentions. A sense of self must begin with an awareness of the fact of one's existence in the world and among other existences. Its development seems to depend on a contemplation and experiencing of ideas and phenomena that widen and deepen consciousness so that the personal realm referred to above comes into being and the conception of being a particular person is formed.

Much can go wrong in the development of self. This is clear from the great variety of ways in which the concept of the self can be used in moral and social appraisal, ranging from severe disapproval of those we characterize as 'self-centred' to warm approval of the person who 'puts her whole self into everything she does'. In seeking to consolidate a moral self it is easy to fall into error, attempting to find a particularity for oneself by cultivating an idiosyncratic personality that concentrates on self-expression and excessive introspection. This is to mistake an empty individualism for the moral self-possession that is desired, and seems to result in loneliness and loss of meaning. This may be because thought has not been given to the implications of the well-known piece of perennial wisdom that tells us that we must lose the self before we can find it. The losing of self that seems to be required by that injunction is that which occurs through a disinterested concern with matters outside oneself. This concern is not of the kind that operates on a situation in order to achieve some end or which gathers material with which to adorn one's individualism, but one which affects the mind and character because one has become absorbed in the contemplation of something without thought of its implications for oneself. This is the loss of self that is required. Through this kind of concern one imaginatively, laboriously, inhabits another segment of reality; the self is lost in absorption in what is contemplated and subsequently is found, its understanding much augmented by the experience it has undergone. And this is simply another aspect of that attentive seeing, already referred to, that has been suggested as the basis of moral being and from which understanding, sympathy, social concern and fair judgement can follow.

4   REFLECTING ON SUICIDE

If we now reflect on the moral issues of suicide in the kind of context just outlined we must begin, we know, from within the milieu of our inherited traditions and attitudes. We shall recognize that there are numerous and often disparate views of suicide, that we are not familiar with all of them, and that there exist or have existed practices and beliefs, such as seppuku and suttee, that are difficult to understand and even, in some cases, difficult to see as credible. And perhaps what we are most immediately aware of is not so much a range of arguments for and against the moral justification of suicide as what was described in an earlier chapter as the natural instinct to preserve life, one's own and that of others, that shows itself in a spontaneous aversion from thoughts of self-inflicted death. Thus there are both traditional and natural elements on which to reflect and on which to exercise moral imagination in order to acquire, in relation to suicide, what Kekes describes as a

breadth of moral sensitivity. This exercise of moral imagination includes that open attentiveness which enables one to
appraise a matter. It allows one to recognize, for example,
that a self-killing that shocks may also be understood as a
dignified realization of the personal ideals of the one who
dies and that courage or vision or nobility, perhaps all three,
have been exercised in achieving them. The consideration
of a particular instance of suicide will dwell on whether the
person concerned had been revengeful, malicious, feckless,
courageous, thoughtful, had been true to his religious and
moral convictions, behaved justly and so on. These thoughts
on the self-killings of others will relate back to what moral
possibilities there are for onself, and to how one might
characterize one's attitude to one's own death and to the
possibility of bringing it about for oneself. But a person
who reflects in this way will not, I suggest, be one who
readily takes to self-killing. Revengeful and malicious suicide
would be ruled out. The suicide of a good person would be
one that exhibited virtues and that was consistent with the
person's moral ideals for her life and character and with her
understanding of the moral tradition that enabled her to
form those ideals. From the basis of this kind of reflection
it should be possible to approach the broader moral questions
about suicide, questions about its justification and rationality
and about the kind of statement or judgement made by a
person's commission of it.

5   A NATURAL METAPHYSICS

In the preceding sections I have begun to give an account
of moral activity that retains what I saw as valuable in
existentialist thought and that tries to remedy some of its
deficiencies. I suggested that what in existentialism is valuable
for a conception of morality is its emphasis on responsibility
and self, and on the thought that we make values. Those
particular elements of existentialism show up as especially
important in thinking about suicide, since suicide is both a
personal and an ultimate act, reflection upon which invites
questions about the self and about the value and meaning

of life. I rejected the essential existentialist tenet that each person either makes values afresh through being authentic or else acts inauthentically and thereby becomes thing-like, and suggested instead that one's morality is not made on the basis of nothing but is derived in part from tradition and education, in part from reflection and the use of moral imagination: that we both discover and make our morality and that actions are not chosen without grounds but follow from the kind of person one is; that at best our actions have a kind of necessity or inevitability.

What was also seen as valuable in Sartrean existentialism was that it offers a metaphysical perspective for thinking about suicide and although one may not want to accept its particular perspective, metaphysical speculation in relation to suicide cannot be ignored. It is readily generated by reflection on suicide because thoughts about the ending of a life raise questions not only about the meaning and value of that particular life but of life or existence in general. For those with a religious faith a metaphysical perspective is provided by that faith. For those without one, the thought of an adherence to one of the great metaphysical systems of the past usually holds little attraction because it too closely resembles a position of faith. However, there does seem to be a way of deepening moral thought and meaning without recourse to the positing of a system that is ultimate or beyond experience. The way is to look rather more carefully at what we have within the life of the natural world. One might call this a kind of moral naturalism, or a natural metaphysics. It requires that we become more aware of the illimitableness of the moral concepts we use, concepts such as love, justice, courage, loyalty, humility, and so on, and which are as much natural features of the lives of human beings who strive to live well as are the concepts that have to do with work, education, sociability, exploration and art. In discussing a similar line of thought Iris Murdoch has suggested that the concept of Good is both ultimately indefinable and mysterious. She writes: 'One might say that true morality is a sort of unesoteric mysticism, having its source in an austere and unconsoled love of the Good'.[10] Good, she suggests, may be seen both as an ideal to which we aspire and as a term that is sometimes applicable to our attempts to achieve the ideal; it has a unifying power for our understanding of the kinds of concepts already mentioned – work, art, education and so on; it lets us see the relationships between these concepts; it invites contemplation of concepts that have affinities with Good, concepts such as perfection, reason and reality; and it enables us to extend our thinking about the innumerable ways in which particular virtues and character-traits contribute to the ideals we formulate for ourselves.

A natural metaphysics of this kind will not ignore those concerns which, it was suggested in Chapter Two, have always been part of the background to reflection about suicide: human nature, the mystery of the source of all things, and the transience of earthly life. It is able to recognize the significance of these concerns, their endurance in human thought, and also the effect, produced by dwelling on them, of staying the impulse to suicide. For it is a propensity of human nature to preserve and foster life, and we do not easily go against something that is both a feature of our human nature and that is generally held to be morally good as well. A natural metaphysics can acknowledge and give weight to this affirmation of the value of life. It can also acknowledge our propensity to reflect on the mystery of the source of all things and the importance in developing moral concepts and in forming an attitude towards suicide of our consciousness of the uncertainties and ambiguities of the relationship in which we stand to the rest of the universe. Our awareness of the transience of earthly life is similarly important in moral reflection and perhaps the most significant and influential element in a natural metaphysics. It reminds us that in thinking about moral goodness we must confront the fact of death. In this connection Iris Murdoch writes: 'Goodness is connected with the acceptance of real death and real chance and real transience and only against the background of this acceptance, which is psychologically so difficult, can we understand the full extent of what virtue is like'.[11]

It does seem to be the case that it is by reflecting partly upon these difficult and often vague concerns, partly upon

particular instances of self-killing that we formulate our
views on suicide. Although suicide has social effects – it
certainly does not lack a public dimension – much of its
morality is of a personal and particular kind and once one
has formed a general attitude to suicide by reflection on
one's moral tradition and on natural human propensities and
virtues, only careful attention to quite specific and individual
features of the circumstances of a suicide or a contemplated
suicide can yield anything approaching a just understanding
of them. This is not a new or remarkable conclusion to
reach, but the discussions of the preceding chapters should
suggest that it is a necessary one.

6   DYING WELL

A person who endeavours to live well, to achieve moral
sensitivity and develop virtues of character and action will
also wish to die well. And if it is the case, as has been
maintained in some of the arguments presented in this book,
that there are circumstances in which self-killing is rational,
justifiable, honourable and commendable, then it is entirely
feasible that ending one's life for oneself might be a way of
securing a good death. It does, for example, seem pointless
that one should have to linger on if one has lost all friends,
family, interests and vigour and wishes only that life will
end before increasing physical disabilities have eroded all
one's dignity and independence.

   In recent years, dramatic advances in the medical technology that works to prolong life have made us much more
sharply aware of the need to think carefully about questions
concerning the possibility of choosing when and how one's
life might end. We are aware, too, of the agonized weighing
of moral issues that takes place in trying to reach a decision
about the switching-off of the life-support machine of a
person who is declared brain-dead. And what becomes clear
in reflecting on these matters is that a person's death, as the
many discussions about what is to count as brain-death have
shown, should not be seen only as the brief single event it
sometimes is, but as something that may take place over a

period of time; as a process that may be gradual and also as one that may, if we wish, be determined to some extent by individual choices.

It seems entirely rational, sane, altruistic, sensitive and dignified to want to die well and to want to secure a good death for oneself in lonely old age or infirmity or under comparable conditions; and it seems irrational, unjust and insensitive that someone who wanted to make such arrangements for themselves should be prevented from doing so. In the same vein, it is unthinkable that anyone, however aged or infirm, should ever feel under any obligation to consider bringing about her or his own death simply in virtue of its being a moral and legal possibility. But there are numerous problems that stand in the way of guaranteeing the personal freedom and autonomy that must be the overriding concern in these matters. For although the acceptability and acceptance of the idea of choosing how one shall die may be regarded as a peak of achievement in self-determination and personal autonomy, it is also a peak from which there is a slippery slope that is able to take us very rapidly downwards to a state of affairs that would be totally repugnant to most people. The slope begins to take us down once it is recognized that someone who wishes to end her life is physically unable to do so: it may be that she is confined to bed and so cannot reach the drug she requires or, even if what she wants is near to hand, that she cannot actually administer the drug without help because she is paralysed. If, when all things have been considered and discussed, it is seen as wrong to prevent a desired death of this kind, assisted suicide might become legally permissible under certain conditions. From there society might move to sanctioning voluntary euthanasia for the infirm and so to producing legislation that would permit authorized medical practitioners to bring to an end the lives of those who had requested such deaths. And even though every innovation and change of both attitude and legislation in these developments has its ground in principles of respect for personal autonomy and care for the well-being of others, it is clear that the legislation allowing for the application of those principles might also allow a government to advocate, facilitate and impose an early and easy death for all who are incapacitated or who make more than usual demands on resources: involuntary or imposed euthanasia could become the norm. What I have described as 'the slippery slope' might bring us to this state of affairs. Once there, our situation is as morally different and distinct from the peak of personal freedom and autonomy as if we were separated from it by a wide chasm.

The Nazi policies and practices of the 1930s vividly remind us that any concern about abuse of the legislation that allows for choosing one's death is not just theoretical. Nor does that concern relate only to past events and policies. A paper written by Robert Kastenbaum in 1976 and called 'Suicide as the preferred way of death' reveals how easily an unscrupulous and opportunist pragmatism may take advantage of legislation derived from humane moral principles. Kastenbaum starts by suggesting that 'within a few years suicide will not be regarded as crime, weakness, failure or pathology . . . it will have become the model, ideal or preferred mode of death in our society'.[12] Referring to the American way of death he remarks that 'we do have in our society a fairly decisive preference for the quick and easy death (exceptions readily granted). Suicide, then, can recommend itself as a way to achieve this desired ending'.[13] And he reminds us of the changing attitudes of churchmen and theologians and of the general revision of attitudes towards abortion, voluntary euthanasia and suicide. He then looks at what he calls 'pragmatic sanction for death' and in this context cites the views of Walter W. Sackett, a physician and also a member of the Florida legislature who introduced a bill favouring euthanasia and who, Kastenbaum writes, 'has spoken of the desirability of conserving public resources by discontinuing the existence of deeply retarded state wards . . . has indicated that those in a chronic and hopeless situation should not be supported . . . argues for the merciful discontinuation of life of the aged . . . claims that many elders fully support this approach, fearing prolonged dying more than death *per se*'.[14] He remarks of Sackett's view that it is 'but a logical extension of well established tendencies in our society to allocate life-support resources according to certain priorities . . . what he offers is quite in keeping with our inclination to select some lives for safeguarding and support, others for hazard and death'.[15]

What has happened here? The views and proposals expressed in the paper pay no more than lip-service to the principle of respecting personal and individual wishes. The reasonable thought that some kinds of suicide are acceptable is conflated with the advocacy of the imposed deaths of the senile, the infirm and the helpless, and a picture is offered of a society in which the voluntary termination of life is institutionalized, expected and approved of as being socially valuable. That picture is morally repulsive. It pays almost no attention to the concerns and wishes of individual persons. It ignores the fact that to institutionalize suicide and voluntary euthanasia would render them unacceptable in that it would remove all possibility of their being autonomously and freely chosen. And it does not even question the morality of developing a culture that would regard elders and others as unproductive and expendable.

It may well be that to end one's own life, under certain conditions, will come to be seen as an entirely acceptable way of bringing about a good death for oneself. Similarly, certain forms of assisted suicide and voluntary euthanasia may eventually be legalized in order that it can be open to everyone to exercise the entitlement to declare a value for their lives and to choose how they will end them. But if all this is to come about, much careful thought will have to be given not only to the moral issues arising from the actions themselves but also to finding ways of preventing the exercise of the kinds of social policies enunciated in Kastenbaum's paper. Moreover, when assisted suicide and euthanasia are under consideration, certain moral issues arise that have no part in discussions of wholly autonomous suicide. These issues are acute. They have to do with the involvement of another person or persons in the bringing about of the deaths of those who request euthanasia or of those who wish to end their lives but who cannot, without help, procure the means to do so.

NOTES

1 Sartre (1953), *op. cit.*, p. 627.
2 *Ibid.*
3 Kekes, John (1984) 'Moral Sensitivity', *Philosophy*, 59, no. 227, p. 10.
4 *Ibid.*, p. 8.
5 *Ibid.*, p. 12.
6 Murdoch, I. (1970) *The Sovereignty of Good*, Routledge & Kegan Paul, p. 34.
7 *Ibid.*, p. 40.
8 Wittgenstein, L. (1965) 'Lecture on Ethics' (1929/30) *Philosophical Review*, 74, p. 7.
9 Kekes, *op. cit.*, p. 8.
10 Murdoch, *op. cit.*, p. 92.
11 *Ibid.*, p. 103.
12 Kastenbaum, R. (1976) 'Suicide as the preferred way of death', in Schneidman, E. S. (ed.), *Suicidology: Contemporary Developments*, Grune & Stratton, p. 425.
13 *Ibid.*, pp. 430–1.
14 *Ibid.*, p. 435.
15 *Ibid.*, pp. 435–6.

CHAPTER SIX

Killing and letting die

1 EUTHANASIA: DEFINITIONS AND DISTINCTIONS

In moving from suicide to euthanasia we move from what is normally a private affair to something which is essentially more public. An act of euthanasia inevitably involves at least two people. In itself this raises issues not raised by suicide. As well as the rationality and morality of any decisions taken by the one who is to die, we must also consider the rationality and morality of the decisions taken by the one who will procure the act of euthanasia. We must also consider the rights and duties of both parties and how they are affected by the nature of the relationship between them.

The *Concise Oxford Dictionary* defines 'euthanasia' as a 'gentle & easy death' and the 'bringing about of this, esp. in cases of incurable & painful disease'. This is clearly incomplete. All sorts of murders might be procured in ways which were 'gentle and easy' without there being the slightest temptation to call them acts of euthanasia.

What is required to differentiate euthanasia from straight-forward murder is, as Philippa Foot points out,[1] the qualification that the killing be done 'for the sake of the one who is to die'. This may not accord with certain historical usages, but it fits fairly well with the way most would use the word now. It also has the advantage, whilst not being entirely morally neutral, of not begging the question in favour of the moral justifiability of euthanasia from the beginning.

What the qualification lays stress on is the motives and intentions of the one who kills. This seems right. What distinguishes cases which are more or less uncontroversially murders from those about which, though they are clearly killings, there is some doubt, is the presence or the absence of the intention to benefit the one who dies.

Take the case of Charlotte Hough who (as reported in *The Sunday Times* of 22 June 1986) promised an elderly woman that she would stay with her throughout a suicide attempt and, if necessary, make sure that she was really dead. When the woman's cocktail of pills apparently did not work, Charlotte Hough, reluctantly complying with the old woman's emphatic prior instructions, placed a plastic bag over her head. She did not want to, and had hoped that she would not have to when she first agreed to be with the old woman until she died. Charlotte Hough was found guilty of attempted murder and served six months of a nine-month sentence.

Probably most people would be uncertain about how they should react morally to such a case, even though in most legal jurisdictions it would be murder, given that the facts were never in dispute. The uncertainty is due to the fact that Charlotte Hough acted out of a sense of concern for the old lady. She felt obliged to keep the promise she had reluctantly made and to respect the old lady's wishes.

We may contrast this with the case of *Bonnyman* (1942) (28 *Cr. App. Rep.* 131). Bonnyman was a doctor who realized that his wife was exhibiting all the symptoms of diabetes, and he refrained from telling her. Thinking that she merely had a particularly bad bout of influenza, she did not seek treatment and died. At best it seems he simply did not care whether she lived or died; at worst he may actually have wanted her out of the way. No stretching of the imagination could see this as a case of euthanasia. Either Bonnyman's wife's welfare did not weigh with him at all, or else he actively wished her ill.

Another obvious distinction between Hough and Bonnyman is consent. The old woman did not just consent, she begged Charlotte Hough to help her. Dr Bonnyman's wife did not merely not consent, she was (presumably deliberately) kept in ignorance of what faced her. Normally we take it that people are the best judges of their own interests and this is why, in so many circumstances, consent is so important.

In the case of euthanasia there are three ways in which consent can figure: voluntary, involuntary and non-voluntary euthanasia. Typically euthanasia would be said to be *voluntary* if it were carried out at the victim's request (as in Hough's case). There are, of course, bound to be problems about whether the request was entirely uncoerced and rationally made, and in some cases these may be irresolvable. But some cases will be clear enough. We have seen from the discussion of suicide that wanting to die is not necessarily an irrational thing to want.

If someone does not explicitly request euthanasia this does not mean that they do not want it; it would be reasonable, however, to assume that they do not. Euthanasia in such a case would be *involuntary*, and, even more obviously, it would be if someone had clearly expressed a wish to live as long as possible, whatever the circumstances.

There is a third category which is in many ways the most important. Newborn babies do not yet have, and comatose or severely brain-damaged adults have lost, the capacity to request or refuse euthanasia. In such cases neither consent nor the lack of it can be said to be a factor, so euthanasia, if considered, could be neither voluntary nor involuntary, but *non-voluntary*. This suggests that consent is not *the* fundamental issue for no one believes that whether severely damaged and disabled adults and newborn babies are killed simply does not matter. Consent is also not fundamental in the sense that merely because they consent to euthanasia it does not entitle you to kill someone; just as their consenting to be harmed does not entitle you to harm someone.

Besides the issue of consent, there is also the often made distinction between *active* and *passive* euthanasia, and whether it matters morally which is involved. On the face of it, it would seem that it does, for had Charlotte Hough simply sat with the old lady until she died, then it is hard to see how she could have been convicted of attempted murder. She herself stated that she was quite prepared just to sit with the old lady, talk to her and perhaps pray with her until the end. She found it extremely difficult, however, to actually put the plastic bag over the old lady's head, knowing what that would mean. Many would feel the same. It does not seem that just sitting back and letting death happen is all right, whereas actively bringing death about is wrong. Dr Bonnyman just watched his wife die, and no one would think any the better of him for that.

There are, however, many doctors who believe that passive euthanasia is morally (and legally) preferable to active euthanasia, and that whereas the latter is never permissible, the former sometimes is. This belief has been attacked by philosophers who cannot see that it makes any moral difference at all whether death is caused by someone doing something to bring it about, or someone not doing anything to prevent its coming about. The distinction between active and passive euthanasia is therefore of great practical as well as theoretical importance.

In this chapter and Chapter Seven we will consider the distinction between active and passive euthanasia and whether it, or something like it, can be rescued from the criticisms of those who do not see it as having any moral significance. The question of whether it can ever be right to bring about the death of someone who does not want to die will be taken up in Chapter Eight. But before addressing the discussion itself the reader will benefit from its being set in an historical and legal context.

2   AN HISTORICAL AND LEGAL NOTE

It is impossible in the space available to do full justice to the complexities of the law and to the history of thought about euthanasia; in any case, much of that history has already been discussed in Chapter Two in relation to suicide.

Not all cultural traditions are as antithetical to the idea of euthanasia as our Western tradition apparently is. Kuhse and Singer even argue that ours is a deviant tradition, particularly in its attitude to benevolent infanticide:

Most cross-cultural studies of non-Western societies have found that the majority accepted infanticide in at least some circumstances. For instance, a sample compiled by C. Ford . . . found that of 64 societies, only 19 expressly forbade infanticide. A later study by J. W. Whiting examines 88 societies; infanticide was practised in 71 of them . . . Moreover the investigators were inclined to believe that this *underestimated* the prevalence of infanticide, since many societies which claimed not to follow the practice had considerably more male than female children.[2]

There is, however, evidence for thinking that even our Western tradition is less homogeneous in its thought on this matter than might first appear. The Graeco-Roman tradition sustained very varied views on euthanasia and, as we have already seen in Chapter Two, pp. 22–3, on suicide. For though both Plato and Aristotle condemned suicide, Plato supported infanticide for defective infants in the *Republic:*

> It follows from our former admissions . . . that the best men must cohabit with the best women in as many cases as possible and the worst with the worst in the fewest, and that the offspring of the one must be reared and that of the other not, if the flock is to be as perfect as possible.[3]

> But when . . . the men and the women have passed the age of lawful procreation, we shall leave [them] free to form such relationships with whomsoever they please . . . first admonishing them preferably not even to bring to light anything whatever thus conceived, but if they are unable to prevent a birth to dispose of it on the understanding that we cannot rear such an offspring.[4]

And Aristotle makes a similar proposal in the *Politics:*

> With regard to the choice between abandoning an infant or rearing it let it be lawful that no cripple child be reared.[5]

The Romans, like many other cultures which set a high premium on honour, saw suicide as an honourable course in certain circumstances (see Chapter Two, p. 22). Seneca wrote:

> I will not relinquish old age if it leaves my better part intact. But if it begins to shake my mind, if it destroys my faculties one by one, if it leaves me not life but breath, I will depart

from the putrid or the tottering edifice. If I know that I must suffer without hope of relief I will depart not through fear of the pain but because it prevents all for which I would live.[6]

It is generally acknowledged that the coming of Christianity changed this picture radically. Early Christians were pacifists and were resolutely opposed to all forms of killing, though Augustine's appeal was to Mosaic Law in the form of the sixth commandment and much in what is held to be a distinctively Christian position on killing is actually Judaic in origin.[7] None the less, whilst Judaic law forbids euthanasia, it allows that '. . . you may, under special circumstances of suffering and helplessness, allow death to come'.[8] Similarly the Roman Catholic Church, whilst unwavering in its condemnation of euthanasia and suicide, allows that in certain circumstances 'extraordinary means' of prolonging life need not be employed.[9] Even Thomas More, who was a notable Roman Catholic of his time and was executed for his refusal to deny the supremacy of the Pope and was subsequently canonized, was able in 1515 to write the following in his *Utopia*:

> Such as be sick of incurable diseases they comfort . . . But if the disease be not only incurable, but also full of continual pain and anguish; then the priests and the magistrates exhort the man, seeing he is not able to do any duty of life, and by overliving his life is noisome and irksome to other, and grievous to himself, that he will not be unwilling to die, but rather take a good hope to him, and either despatch himself out of that painful life, as out of prison, or a rack of torment, or else suffer himself willingly to be rid of it by other. And in so doing they tell him that he shall do wisely, seeing by his death he shall lose no commodity, but end his pain. And because in that act he shall follow the counsel of the priests, that is to say, of the interpreters of God's will and pleasure, they show him that he shall do like a godly and virtuous man.[10]

This patchwork of apparently inconsistent viewpoints is reflected too in our current law. In both the UK and the USA the law recognizes no difference between euthanasia and any other form of killing.[11] Because motive forms no part of the definition of murder in either jurisdiction, intentional killing, even from benevolent motives, by a fully competent adult would have to count as murder. (The phrase 'with malice aforethought' is a term of legal art and simply means 'with full knowledge of and intending the consequences of one's actions'.) The practice of the law is, however, significantly different from what the theory might suggest. Ruth Russell[12] has shown that of sixteen cases of direct, active euthanasia by non-doctors tried and widely publicized in the USA between 1832 and 1973, only two resulted in murder convictions (and neither resulted in execution: one received life imprisonment, the other, life parole). Of the remaining fourteen cases, two were convicted on a lesser charge than first degree murder, four were acquitted, six were acquitted on the grounds of 'temporary insanity' and in two cases the court refused to indict. Russell was only able to find eight cases world-wide of mercy-killings by doctors which resulted in their being brought to trial. Of these, two were convicted of a lesser charge than murder, five were acquitted and in one case the court refused to indict. We may conjecture, though of course cannot prove, that many more such cases never come to trial.

On passive euthanasia the law is, perhaps understandably, more complex. The cases of *Arthur* and *Baby Doe* will be discussed below (section 3), but it is worth rehearsing here four examples put to the jury by the judge in the Arthur trial whilst directing them as to the law:

1   A Down's syndrome child is born with an intestinal obstruction. If the obstruction is not removed, the child will die. Here . . . the surgeon might say: 'As this child is a mongol . . . I do not propose to operate; I shall allow nature to take its course'. No one could say that the surgeon was committing an act of murder by declining to take a course which would save the child.

2   A severely handicapped child, who is not otherwise going to die, is given a drug in such amounts that the drug itself will cause death. If the doctor acts intentionally then it would be open to the jury to say: yes, he was killing, he was murdering that child.

3   A patient is afflicted with terminal cancer and is suffering great pain. Increasing doses of pain-killing drugs are required to alleviate the patient's distress. The point will be reached where the pain-killing drug will cause the patient's death. This is a case which could never be murder. That was a proper practice of medicine.

4   A child, afflicted by an irreversible handicap and rejected by its mother, contracts pneumonia. If, in this case, the doctor withheld antibiotics and by a merciful dispensation of providence the child died, then it would be very unlikely . . . that you (or any other jury) would say that the doctor was committing murder.[13]

It is hard to see what principle distinguishes (2) from the rest. Only in (3) is the patient already dying; in (1) and (3) the child is disabled just as in (2). The only discernible difference is that in (1) and (4) the doctor's inaction causes the death and in (3) the death is, arguably, not directly intended. Only in (2) is the death intended as the result of something the doctor actually *does*. But we have already seen that causing death through inaction rather than action does not necessarily render you either morally or legally innocent of responsibility for that death. The trial judge may be right in his intuitions about what is and is not murder, but the jury must have found it very hard indeed to extract any real guidance from his examples.

United States law is no clearer. The celebrated case of Karen Quinlan (1976) seems to establish the principle that if death resulted from treatment being discontinued, this would not be illegal: 'We believe . . . that the ensuing death would not be homicide but rather expiration from existing natural causes'.[14] This judgement was based partly on an individual's right to decline treatment but was complicated by the fact that Karen Quinlan's chances of recovery were extremely poor and that she was not competent to exercise that right for herself. It was her father who asked for treatment to be discontinued. In cases involving children US law has taken a rather different view. The case of *Baby Doe* will be discussed below. In the case of *Maine Medical Center v. Houle* (1974) the court ruled that the parents' wish that treatment not be undertaken should not be upheld: 'In the court's opinion the issue before the court is not the prospective quality of the life to be preserved, but the medical feasibility of the proposed treatment compared with the almost certain risk of death should treatment be withheld.'[15]

There is, therefore, a very real and currently unresolved question as to when and in what circumstances a doctor may cease to provide life-sustaining medical procedures. It seems unlikely that the law can resolve this problem since lawyers seem to be afflicted by the very same moral and conceptual uncertainties that the rest of us face in considering such cases. The extent to which courts, in interpreting general laws for specific cases, rely on moral intuitions which are themselves both unclear and debatable suggests that we must attack the moral confusions before we have any hope of sorting out the law.

3 'NURSING CARE ONLY'

It is said that in coronary care units the letters ONTR (orders not to resuscitate) may sometimes be found on patients' notes.[16] A. H. Clough's couplet:

> Thou shalt not kill: but needst not strive
> Officiously to keep alive.

has been quoted in defence of such procedures (though in apparent ignorance of Clough's satirical intent).[17] In an article in *New Society*[18] Andrew Bell, a researcher who worked on a television documentary about euthanasia, said of the distinction between active and passive euthanasia:

> For most British doctors this distinction is crucial, marking out the ethical boundary between recognising that human life is finite and acting as executioner.

In England in 1981, Dr Leonard Arthur was tried at Leicester Crown Court for the attempted murder of John Pearson, a Down's syndrome baby. John's mother is reported to have said 'I don't want him, love' to her husband, and Arthur, having overheard the remark, ordered 'nursing care only' for the child. This meant that John Pearson was kept comfortable, fed with water and sedated. He died sixty-nine hours after his birth.[19]

At Arthur's trial a number of eminent witnesses testified that giving 'nursing care only' to severely disabled and unwanted babies was accepted paediatric practice. They said:

> No paediatrician takes life; but we accept that allowing babies to die – and I know the distinction is narrow, but we all feel it tremendously profoundly – it is in the baby's interests at times.[20]

> There is an important difference between allowing a child to die and taking action to kill it.[21]

> I distinguish between allowing to die and killing. It is a distinction that is somewhat difficult to defend in logic, but I agree it is good medical practice not to take positive steps to end life.[22]

This attitude is not peculiar to the UK. In 1973, Duff and Campbell[23] revealed that in a New England special care nursery, severely disabled infants were often, with the consent of the parents, allowed to die. The American Medical Association has stated that:

> The cessation of the employment of extraordinary means to prolong the life of the body when there is irrefutable evidence that biological death is imminent is the decision of the patient and/or his immediate family.[24]

The case of Baby Doe, born 9 April 1982 in Bloomington Hospital, Indiana, USA, would seem to confirm Duff and Campbell's observations and also to go rather further than the AMA guidelines.[25] Like John Pearson, Baby Doe's death was imminent only in the sense that it was proposed not to offer it life-saving treatment. Baby Doe's parents agreed that it was in the child's best interests for it not to be treated but, instead, simply to be kept comfortable and pain-free. They were aware that, if this course were followed, Baby Doe would not survive. The parents' right to opt for this for their child was confirmed by the Monroe County Court and upheld on appeal by the Indiana Supreme Court. Appeals to the US Supreme Court were in train when Baby Doe died on 14 April.

By definition, the Arthur decision shows that, in English law, what Dr Arthur did was legal. What is less clear is what exactly that was and what, consequently, the decision does or does not permit doctors to do in the future. The case of *In Re B. (a minor)*(1981)[26] demonstrates the problem, for in this case an injunction was obtained requiring B., an infant suffering from Down's syndrome and intestinal obstruction which needed surgery, to be treated. United States law is in similar disarray as shown by the Baby Doe case.

There does seem to be a *prima facie* moral difference between killing someone and letting them die. Not jumping into the canal to save someone from drowning (assuming that you could) may be reprehensible but does not seem, on the face of it, to be morally equivalent to pushing them in in the first place, intending them to drown. Whether paediatricians should allow certain babies to die is a question we have yet to address but, initially at least, it does look like a very different question from that of whether paediatricians should be allowed to kill those babies.

4   'ACTIVE AND PASSIVE EUTHANASIA'

In a highly influential paper published in 1975, James Rachels argued that 'the bare difference between killing and letting die does not, in itself, make a moral difference'.[27] On the contrary, he suggested that in many actual cases, opting for passive euthanasia actually produced a worse outcome than a policy of active euthanasia would have. He offers four reasons against what he takes to be the conventional doctrine and, in view of the centrality of Rachels's views in the subsequent discussion, it is worth looking at them in some detail.

1   A policy of passive euthanasia normally takes longer to bring about death than active euthanasia would have. If the patient is in pain or discomfort and especially if the pain or

suffering is part of the reason for opting for euthanasia then it is either cruel or cruel *and* inconsistent to opt for a policy which brings about more suffering that at least one of the available alternatives.

2   Some Down's syndrome children are born with additional complications such as an intestinal obstruction. If they are given 'nursing care only' then it is often the complication which causes their death. (There is no treatment for Down's syndrome, which is not, in any case, a fatal condition.) The policy of 'nursing care only' is never adopted for children who suffer from such complications alone. It is the Down's syndrome, therefore, which is presumably the reason for opting for 'nursing care only'. But the choice of which babies die and which do not is being made to turn on the additional defects. The policy of allowing some babies to die is therefore being made, in effect, on grounds which are irrelevant to the decision, namely whether the baby also happens to suffer from another defect or contracts a secondary illness.

3   The distinction between killing and letting die, in itself, bears no moral weight. Smith and Jones both stand to gain a lot of money when their six-year old cousin dies. They plan, separately, to kill him. If we suppose two cases, then in the first, Smith gets to him first while he is in the bath and holds his head under the water until he dies. In the second, Jones gets to him first but, before he can drown him, the child slips, bangs his head and falls, unconscious, with his head under the water. Jones waits, ready to hold his head under the water should the child recover, but this proves unnecessary. Smith drowns the child; Jones lets him drown when he could have saved him. Both Smith and Jones are murderers, both are equally morally culpable. If there is ever a difference between the moral seriousness of a killing and a letting die, then it cannot lie simply in the fact that one is a killing and the other a letting die, it must lie in some other feature of the cases.

4   The argument in favour of a moral difference in causal responsibility for acts on the one hand and omissions on the

other, is invalid. It is not true that when a doctor allows a patient to die he does nothing and hence, *a fortiori*, nothing for which he can be blamed. There is at least one thing he does – he lets the patient die. If the patient were suffering from a curable condition and was otherwise healthy, and the doctor declined to give treatment easily within his power to give, then the doctor would be responsible, both causally and morally, for that patient's death. If we feel different about a case where the patient's condition is such that it would be better for him to die, then it can only be because we do not disapprove of the death, not because we do not believe that the doctor is responsible for it.

Rachels's arguments have prompted an enormous literature in response, both positive and negative. As Rachels himself points out, these arguments have, in themselves, no direct consequence for the morality of euthanasia. For even if he is right that there is no moral significance in whether a death is brought about actively or passively, then the question of whether we may bring that death about at all is still open. Those for whom Rachels's conclusions are uncomfortable are those who believe either:

(a) that active euthanasia is wrong but passive euthanasia is allowable; or
(b) that killing someone amounts to euthanasia and is wrong, but merely letting them die is not euthanasia and is not (always) wrong.

(For our purposes the difference between (a) and (b) can be taken to be merely terminological – nothing substantial separates them.)

Such middle ground between the pro-euthanasiasts and the anti-euthanasiasts seems effectively closed off by Rachels's arguments. In particular, the *prima facie* obviousness of the intuitions mentioned at the end of section 3 (p. 131, above) seems to be rebutted if Rachels is right; it would follow that there is not necessarily any moral difference between killing someone and letting them die. Rachels's argument does, therefore, seem to have important consequences for what we have seen is held by many to be standard paediatric practice. If he is right, it cannot be permissible to allow severely disabled infants to die (whether from their disability or from an intervening illness) unless it is also permissible to kill them directly.

We face, then, either advocating a policy of active euthanasia in such cases, or else one of strenuous and unremitting medical intervention right up to the point where unavoidable death releases us from our obligation to continue to treat. It is not an objection, still less a solution, to this dilemma that active euthanasia is currently, under both UK and US law, illegal, for if active euthanasia is, in certain cases, perfectly moral then we ought to be campaigning for its legalization in those cases. If it is immoral then we ought to be campaigning for the absolute prohibition of passive euthanasia too.[28]

This is not a comfortable choice except for those who would approve of active euthanasia (in some cases). The absolute prohibition of what we have called passive euthanasia – namely, allowing patients to die in circumstances in which we could prolong their lives, however briefly – is not an attractive proposition.

> . . . a doctor aged sixty-eight dying of an inoperable cancer of the stomach. First it was treated by palliative removal of part of the stomach. Shortly afterwards the patient developed a pulmonary embolism and this was removed by an operation. Again he collapsed with myocardial infarction and was revived by the cardiac resuscitation team. His heart stopped on four subsequent occasions and was restarted artificially. The body lingered on for a few more weeks, with severe brain damage following the cardiac arrest and episodes of vomiting accompanied by generalised convulsions.
> This man had been told that he had a stomach cancer; he accepted the diagnosis, which was confirmed by histological examination. Because the cancer had spread to his bones he suffered severe pain that was unrelieved by morphine or pethidine. When his pulmonary embolus was removed he was grateful, but asked that no further attempts should be made to resuscitate him should he require it. The request was not regarded.[29]

A man in his late 50s had been in hospital for eight years on account of advanced Parkinson's disease. During the last year of his life he lost weight progressively, became generally weaker and spent more time in bed. He was less able to talk clearly and needed increasing help with the basic 'activities of daily living'. During this time he had three attacks of bronchitis. The first two were treated with chest physiotherapy and antibiotics. In anticipation of a further attack, it was decided that the man was in fact dying, albeit slowly, and that the next episode of bronchitis would not be treated with physiotherapy and antibiotics but simply symptomatically on the grounds that further curative treatment of the chest infection would, at this stage, be little more than 'resurrecting the man to die again a few weeks later' or 'prescribing a lingering death'. The outcome of a chest infection in these circumstances was quite likely to be the man's death and it was seen as the natural terminal event of the progressive physical deterioration.[30]

To take the view that passive euthanasia – as we have defined it – is never permissible would mean that cases like these ought to be treated with all available medical resources right up to the point when the patient had finally ceased all vital functions. As I indicated in section 2 above (p. 126), even the Roman Catholic Church does not take the view that this kind of response to the terminally ill is always required:

> . . . normally one is held to use only ordinary means . . . that is to say, means that do not involve any grave burden for oneself or another . . . Consequently, if it appears that the attempt at resuscitation constitutes such a burden for the family that one cannot in all conscience impose it upon them, they can lawfully insist that the doctor should discontinue these attempts and the doctor can lawfully comply.[31]

The Pope goes on to say that such a choice would not amount to opting for euthanasia, but it is clear that it amounts to ceasing to do all that might preserve life before life had irrevocably and finally ended. It is, therefore, passive euthanasia according to our definition, though of course nothing much turns on the actual *word* used here. For if Rachels is correct, ceasing extraordinary means of resuscitation is actually morally indistinguishable from actively ending life, and if the former is justified in the circumstances, then so is the latter. Since the latter would, on anyone's definition, count as euthanasia, then so must the former. If Rachels is correct.

Quite a lot hinges on the validity of Rachels's arguments, therefore, and also on their applicability to the views actually expressed. That is to say, Rachels presents himself as criticizing what he calls 'the conventional doctrine'; it matters, therefore, whether there is a unitary conventional doctrine, and whether Rachels correctly represents it, quite as much as it matters whether his criticisms are correct.

5   SOME PROBLEMS WITH RACHELS

The first of Rachels's objections to passive euthanasia is that it is often crueller to let someone die than to kill them. He says that if the death of the patient is already aimed at then surely that aim must be realized as painlessly as possible. But this is to assume that those who advocate that in certain circumstances patients should be allowed to die, are actually aiming at the death of the patient. If my aim is to raise £1000 for charity then it may be that the best (most painless) way of doing this is to steal it from a wealthy but mean acquaintance. She will not miss the money, the charity needs it now, no one else need be coerced into parting with money they would prefer to keep or perhaps cannot really afford. But if my aim is to raise the money I may feel that stealing it is not a means to the end I want to achieve at all. Not, as Rachels seems to want to argue, that it is a means to my end that only my squeamishness or confusion rules out for me.

What is surely implied by the expert witnesses at Arthur's trial is that the aim of 'nursing care only' is *not* to kill the patient, but to let him die. If letting him die is in fact the end that the doctor is aiming at, then killing him is not a way of achieving it. This only fails to make sense if either killing the patient were a better thing to be aiming at than letting him die, and nothing in Rachels's arguments suggests that, or else there is in fact no distinction here worth sticking on. This latter point would be true if letting a patient die were morally equivalent to killing. This is Rachels's third objection, and we will examine it shortly.

His second objection is that where passive euthanasia is favoured, then whether the patient lives or dies will depend on factors which are quite irrelevant to determining whether passive euthanasia is an appropriate course of action. If a Down's syndrome baby is not treated then it will not die because it has Down's syndrome. Down's syndrome babies often suffer other congenital defects – an intestinal malformation called 'duodenal atresia' is one of the commonest. It involves either the narrowing or total absence of the passage between the stomach and the intestine and it means that the sufferer cannot be fed normally. The condition can be remedied by a relatively simple operation with a high success rate, and an otherwise normal child would receive this treatment as standard procedure. A Down's syndrome baby who also suffered from duodenal atresia and for whom 'nursing care only' was ordered, would starve to death, though care would be taken to prevent dehydration and sedatives would normally depress the appetite so that the child felt no hunger. Rachels's objection is that untreated Down's syndrome babies with duodenal atresia who are 'allowed to die' will die because of the duodenal atresia, and not because of the Down's syndrome. If duodenal atresia is not in itself considered a reason for prescribing 'nursing care only', then the babies are not being allowed to die on that account. If on the other hand it is the Down's syndrome which is the reason for allowing them to die then it is inconsistent to allow Down's syndrome babies with duodenal atresia to die, whilst permitting Down's syndrome babies without duodenal atresia to live.

Something does seem to have gone wrong with this policy. 'Nursing care only', as described at the Arthur trial, is not just a matter of not treating life-threatening conditions. It is a regime which no infant, disabled or not, could survive. It is worth asking whether we would be prepared to describe a situation in which a perfectly normal baby was not fed, but given only water and sedatives which depressed the appetite, as one in which that baby was merely 'allowed to die' and not killed. Equally, how would we describe a situation in which an otherwise healthy child who suffered from an intestinal obstruction was not treated for that condition, though treatment was easily available, and died as a consequence?

Why should it be permissible not to treat a Down's syndrome baby with duodenal atresia when not treating a normal baby with duodenal atresia is forbidden? Only, so Rachels would argue, if it is permissible for the Down's syndrome baby to die. But if that is so, then it must be permissible for *any* Down's syndrome baby to die, not just those with duodenal atresia. Alternatively, one may argue that no child with treatable duodenal atresia may be left untreated. But in that case, a Down's syndrome baby with treatable duodenal artesia must be treated, too. Either way, it cannot be that not treating a child with duodenal atresia with the consequences that that child dies, is permissible, whereas killing them is not permissible.

But this does not show that allowing a patient to die through non-treatment is morally equivalent to killing them. At best it shows that non-treatment of a patient who would live if treated is sometimes the moral equivalent of killing them. Is the failure to save someone's life when you could have done so the moral equivalent of killing them when you could have avoided doing so? Rachels's third objection to the distinction between active and passive euthanasia is the claim that this is so.

Rachels's example of Smith and Jones *is* one in which letting someone die seems no better than actually killing them. Smith actually drowns the child for the sake of gaining the inheritance. Jones intends to drown the child for the same reason, but in the event does not have to because the child drowns anyway. Jones, however, could have rescued him from the bath, but does not do so. Both are causally responsible for the child's death in the sense that had either of them acted differently, which they were perfectly able to do, the child would not have died. Both knew this. But causal responsibility is not a sufficient condition for moral responsibility. If you give someone a food to which they suddenly and unexpectedly have an allergic reaction and die, then you are causally responsible in the sense that had you not done what you did they would not have died. You are clearly not *morally* responsible if you did not know, and could not have known, that this would happen. Nor is foreseeing the consequences of your actions sufficient for moral responsibility. If you have an alcoholic friend to whom you owe twenty pounds, you may foresee that giving her the twenty pounds will have disastrous consequences, but that does not make you morally responsible for those consequences if you give her the money. You may feel you have an obligation to mention Alcoholics Anonymous, or to try to persuade her not to hold you to your debt. But these are separate issues. What is sufficient[32] to establish moral responsibility is an intention to bring about just those consequences for which you are causally responsible. Smith and Jones both *intended* to be causally responsible for the child's death, and both succeeded. That is why they are both morally guilty. The difference between the way in which they are both morally responsible is, however, according to some, not without significance. Smith actually *initiates* the causal chain of events which leads to the child's death when he holds the child's head under the bathwater. Jones *permits* a causal chain of events which he did not initiate to continue. He does nothing to stop the unconscious child from drowning in the bath. Thus, though we probably think them equally guilty, we may think them guilty of different things. Jones probably could not be convicted of murder unless he was *in loco parentis* (he had assumed a duty of care for the boy).[33] What he is guilty of is gross and self-serving callousness. This is not normally a criminal offence, not because it cannot be as serious an immorality as murder, but because it would be impossible to prove, except in exceptional circumstances.

Rachels is quite right that *in such a case* there is no difference between knowingly causing an evil and knowingly permitting an evil to take place. But this is surely because both Smith and Jones *intended* that the evil should occur. It would be different if Smith and Jones were simply *reckless*, in the sense that they did not care one way or the other. Smith would still have an obligation to ensure that his actions did not result in anyone's death. Jones would not, in general, have an obligation to ensure that no one died whose life he might have saved. Doctors, however, *are* usually held to have an obligation to ensure that none of their patients dies when they might have been saved. So even if, in general, Rachels is not right to assume that letting someone die is always morally equivalent to actually killing them, it may be that as far as the doctors are concerned, he is. What we need to establish now is whether doctors and other health-care practitioners would actually disagree with him about that. Does anyone, in other words, actually hold the doctrine that Rachels is criticizing?

6   WHAT IS THE DISTINCTION?

At first sight, it would seem that doctors do believe that there is a morally significant difference between active and passive euthanasia which lies in the fact that the former involves directly killing a patient, which is never right, and that the latter involves ceasing to treat a patient whose life might have been saved, which is sometimes right. We have quoted some of these views already (p. 130 above). For example:

> No paediatrician takes life; but we accept that allowing babies to die . . . is in the baby's interests at times.

> There is an important difference between allowing a child to die and taking action to kill it.

> I distinguish between allowing to die and killing.

These quotations do seem to vindicate Rachels's position. It would be unwise, however, to reject the active/passive distinction just yet, for concealed under the language of acts and omissions, talk of 'killings' and 'letting die', there is an important difference of view. There are those who believe that it is permissible to end a baby's life, so long as it would be better for the child that it did not survive. Perhaps they are represented by the above quotations. It should be noted, however, that they are speaking in a court of law, and probably in the belief that the law, as it now stands in the

UK and the USA, prohibits active euthanasia but does not (always) prohibit passive euthanasia. It may well be, in other words, that they do not, in fact, believe that allowing a child to die is *morally* better than killing it; merely that the law prohibits active killing and that a doctor should, wherever possible, seek to act within the law. This is speculation. What is not speculative is that some of those quoted, and others, believe that it is sometimes proper to act with the intention that a baby should not survive.

> I have put a baby on 'nursing care only' on four or five occasions with the intention it should not survive.[34]

Dr John Lorber, an advocate of the selective treatment of spina bifida babies (i.e. of the view that only some, not all, such babies should be treated), explains that:

> The main object of selection is not to avoid treating those who would die early in spite of treatment, but to avoid treating those who would survive with severe handicaps.[35]

These views may be contrasted with the following:

> When maximum treatment was viewed as unacceptable by families and physicians in our unit, there was a growing tendency to seek early death as a management option, to avoid that cruel choice of gradual, often slow, but progressive deterioration of the child who was required under these circumstances in effect to kill himself. Parents and the staff then asked if his dying needed to be prolonged.[36]

By the end of this quotation, we are aware that early death as a 'management option' (an unfortunate phrase, as selective quotation has shown[37]) is being advocated only for those who, in the author's opinion, would die anyway. Now there is considerable scope for uncertainty about whether a patient is in fact dying, as well as conceptual problems about what dying actually consists in. None the less, there is a large gap between believing that it is permissible to cease to treat a patient who is going to die anyway, and believing that it is permissible to cease to treat a patient who is only going to die because of the decision to cease treatment.

What this suggests is that whatever is at issue when doctors talk about the difference between active and passive euthanasia is probably more than the simple distinction between killing and letting die. It is also probably true that doctors themselves disagree about what they mean by these terms. Two distinct positions are emerging, however. The first is that it is better for certain extremely severely damaged children with poor future prospects, that their lives be ended. Commonly, it is suggested that their lives be ended passively, rather than actively, though it may be no more than the present state of the law which prompts this suggestion. However, if this is said because it is believed to be morally consistent, rather than just legally prudent, then Rachels's criticisms would seem to apply to it.

The second position is not so vulnerable to Rachels's arguments. The second quotation (above) is one expression of it. The following, from the Church of England's Board for Social Responsibility, is another:

> In its narrow current sense, euthanasia implies killing, and it is misleading to extend it to cover decisions not to preserve life by artificial means when it would be better for the patient to be allowed to die. Such decisions coupled with a determination to give the patient as good death as possible, may be quite legitimate.[38]

We have also noted the Roman Catholic position that 'normally one is held to use only ordinary means' (above, p. 135). The Roman Catholic Church is also on record as saying that

> . . . the suppression of pain and consciousness by the use of narcotics [is] . . . morally permitted by religion and morality to the doctor and patient (even at the approach of death and if one foresees that the use of narcotics will shorten life) . . . If no other means exist.[39]

Finally we may note the quotation which Rachels himself gives at the beginning of his article as endorsing the distinction he wishes to deny:

> The cessation of the employment of extraordinary means to prolong the life of the body when there is irrefutable evidence that biological death is imminent is the decision of the patient and/or his immediate family. The advice and judgement of

the physician should be freely available to patient and/or his immediate family.[40]

What all these quotations suggest is *not* that it may be permissible to let someone die when you might have saved their life, but that it may be permissible to let someone die if there is little or no hope of saving them. Even then, one may only cease 'extraordinary' or 'artificial' means, or 'maximum' treatment. Certain more basic goods must still be offered to the patient, like, presumably, food, water, narcotics, etc.

So although Rachels is quite right that in themselves there is no moral difference between letting someone die when you could and should have saved them and killing them, this is not what those doctors and theologians we have just quoted seem to have in mind. Why, though, if one may cease, in certain circumstances, to employ 'extraordinary' or 'artificial' means, or offer 'maximum' treatment, may one not, in just those circumstances, kill the patient painlessly? Does Rachels's argument not have some bite, even here?

7   INTENTION AND NEGATIVE RESPONSIBILITY

There are two ways in which we may try to get an opponent to accept our point of view by means of rational argument. The first is to show that it follows by valid argument from premises which we take to be true. But our opponent may not accept that these premises are true. A second tactic overcomes this problem by adopting as premises propositions which our opponent already accepts as true. We then attempt to show that the conclusion follows from those premises. These are arguments *ad hominem* and it is such an argument that Rachels employs. It runs as follows:

1   There are circumstances in which it is permissible to allow someone to·die.
2   Allowing someone to die is morally indistinguishable from killing them. (Because we would agree with Rachels that what Smith and Jones both do is impermissible and

the only thing which distinguishes their actions is that one kills and the other lets someone die.)

3   Therefore killing is permissible in just those cases where letting someone die is permissible.

If we are to deny (3), we must deny either (1) or (2), or both. Since, as we have already seen, most would not wish to deny (1), we must concentrate on (2). Equally, since we have already accepted that the Smith and Jones example shows that, *in that case*, killing is morally indistinguishable from 'letting die', we must turn our attention to the possibility that the cases where we would find 'letting die' acceptable, but killing not, are just not like the Smith and Jones example in some morally significant way. It should be emphasized that, in wanting to deny (3), we do not necessarily want to say that killing is *never* permissible, only to deny that it is always permissible when 'letting die' is permissible. It may be that killing is sometimes permissible, but we shall argue that it is permissible in a much more restricted class of cases than the class of cases in which 'letting die' is permissible. You may, in other words, let someone die in all sorts of cases where it would not be right to kill them, even though there probably are some cases where it would be right to kill them.

It may help us to distinguish Rachels's doctrine from what his opponents consider to be the real distinction if we ask why Rachels believes that it is possible to generalize from Smith and Jones. One reason might be that he believes in the principle of *negative responsibility*. This principle states that one is just as responsible for the consequences of one's inactions as for the consequences of one's actions. The principle is a corollary of *consequentialism*, which is the view that what counts is the consequences of one's actions, not how one acts. Equally, the consequences of one's inactions matter – the fact that they were negative actions rather than positive ones (omissions rather than commissions) does not matter.

If I have an obligation to pay you five pounds then I may give you a five-pound note. Alternatively, I may simply do nothing when someone who owes *me* five pounds gives it to you in error. Similarly, I may steal five pounds from you by taking it out of your purse when you are not looking. But I equally steal five pounds from you if I say and do nothing when it becomes clear that you have totally and permanently forgotten that I owed you five pounds.

Such parallel cases – of actions and inactions which amount to the same – are, however, very tricky to devise. One reason for this is that in order for an action and an inaction to bring about the same state of affairs the background conditions have to be diametrically opposite. Clearly, the conditions under which something may come about through my acting must be very different from the conditions under which the same thing can come about through my inaction. When the background conditions of two cases are so very different it is often hard to see that the final state of affairs is the same. It is not possible, therefore, to draw from a limited number of examples the general conclusion that for any action, there will be an inaction which, if it produces the same consequences, will be its moral equivalent.

In each of the two pairs of cases we have just looked at the intention was the same. It was, in fact, quite difficult to ensure that it was – it would not have been stealing if I had simply not reminded you that I owed you five pounds. It would amount to theft only if it were coupled with a general intention never to remind you. That may be a nice point, but it shows how intention can affect the moral quality of action/inaction even when the consequences are the same. In either acting or refraining from action one may intend to bring about the same thing. However, whilst one normally intends the likely consequences of one's actions, one does not normally intend the likely consequences of one's inactions (there are usually too many of them for that).

Rachels's view is that this makes not the slightest difference. The intention with which an action is done or not done is no more relevant to its moral worth or desirability than whether it is done (or not done) on a Tuesday rather than a Wednesday. He gives this example in support of his view:

> Jack visits his sick and lonely grandmother, and entertains her for the afternoon. He loves her and his only intention is to cheer her up. Jill also visits her grandmother and provides

an afternoon's cheer. But Jill's only concern is that the old lady will soon be making her will; Jill wants to be included among the heirs. Jack also knows that his visit might influence the making of the will, in his favour, but that is not part of his plan. Thus Jack and Jill do the very same thing – they both spend an afternoon cheering up their sick grandmother – and what they do may have the same consequences, namely influencing the will. But their intentions are quite different.[41]

Of this example Rachels says:

The traditional view says that the intention with which an action is done is relevant to determining whether the act is right. The example of Jack and Jill suggests that, on the contrary, the intention is not relevant to assessing whether the act is right or wrong but instead is relevant to assessing the character of the person who does it, which is another thing entirely.[42]

The idea that our moral concern about Jack and Jill attaches in one way to their actions and in quite another to their characters seems bizarre. We would feel no special difficulty about condemning Jill's actions because of the intention with which she performed them. Are we misguided in that? Perhaps the idea is that we should be concerned with what *happens* in the world, and only secondarily, if at all, with people's thoughts about what happens. But this is to misrepresent the connection between actions and intentions, for actions are not mere happenings and intentions not mere thoughts.

We are interested, from the point of view of morals, not in the mere fact that Jack and Jill's granny gets cheered up. Perhaps she's just been watching *Dallas* on the TV and learning that the whole family Ewing has been wiped out by an aerial attack by rogue F-111s has brought a merry smile to her lips. Or maybe the joint spectacle of Jack trying desperately to prove he is not after her money and Jill, equally desperately, trying to conceal the fact that she is, fills her with amusement. Or it is just that the sun is shining, God's in His heaven and all's right with the world. None of these things is of any moral significance because they just *happened*. No one planned them and no one could have stopped them lifting her spirits (because no one knew that they would); they just did. Our moral concern is with *actions* and the *consequences* of actions because we are interested in those aspects of the world which we stand some chance of changing. ('What can't be cured must be endured' is only negative and fatalistic if one is unduly pessimistic about what cannot be cured. What *really* cannot be cured *must* be endured.)

Nor are we especially interested, from a moral perspective, in what Jack and Jill were thinking at the time. They might just as well have been pondering the fate of the Ewings as thinking about what they were doing. We may think about our intentions, but intentions are not thoughts, still less are they just whatever thoughts accompany the action, when we act intentionally. *X* moves her pawn. She intends to win the chess game. Though it is true that she moves her pawn with the intention of winning she has deliberately emptied her mind of all thoughts concerning her wish for victory, her determination to win, etc., because she knows that such thoughts would only distract her from making the complex calculations that are necessary. But must it not be true that *at some time* she formed the thought 'I intend to win'? Not necessarily – she *may* never think about winning or losing, but just about playing the game. None the less she could not *play*, or rather no one could play against her, unless she played with the intention of winning. (That is implicit in its being true that she is 'playing chess' rather than 'playing around with chess pieces', 'messing about', etc.) A cat could never form the thought 'I intend to catch that bird' because it does not have the language in which such a thought could be framed. But a cat could certainly stalk a bird with the intention of catching it. (It could not 'stalk' a bird *without* such an intention.)

Intentions and actions are not distinct from one another in the way that thoughts and happenings are. It is therefore just not possible to be interested in actions but not intentions. For when we describe something as an 'action' (rather than an 'event' or an 'occurrence') some intention or other is built into our description. The possibility of attributing different intentions to someone (from what appeared to be so at the time, or from what they profess) just is the possibility of redescribing their action.

So both Jack and Jill can cheer up their granny without intending to (because granny's being cheered up is something that can just happen without anyone's intending it) but it is not the case that Jill can attempt-to-become-a-beneficiary-in-granny's-will without intending it. Rachels says that Jack and Jill 'do the very same thing – they both spend an afternoon cheering up their sick grandmother'. But Jill in addition does something that Jack does not do – she spends an afternoon trying to get her hands on the old girl's money. Jill's intention is not irrelevant to that. So is Jill's intention irrelevant to deciding whether her act was right or wrong? It depends which act we are talking about. Is Rachels suggesting that it is morally indifferent that Jill spent the afternoon trying to exert undue influence on her grand-mother? That only makes sense if it is supposed that the good achieved by cheering her up outweighed the bad aimed at by Jill. We do not know enough about the example to decide that.

Intentions cannot, therefore, be eliminated as irrelevant distractions – they come in as part of our concern with actions whether we like it or not. Suppose a baby dies whilst in the care of a doctor. Obviously this may *concern* us, but if the baby's death was in no way untoward, our concern ends there. Only if the death occurred *as a result* of something someone did would our concern be reawakened. However, this is by no means enough to settle the question of whether what happened was right or wrong. For, say the child died because of the results of someone's intentional action. The doctor, let us imagine, intentionally prescribed a drug which was toxic in its effects. Though the drug was prescribed intentionally, it was prescribed in the mistaken belief that it was not toxic, i.e. *not* with the intention of killing or harming the child. If the mistaken belief was wholly reasonable (everyone thought it was safe) that may be enough to exonerate the doctor completely. (If not, then we enter the twilight area of recklessness, carelessness, negligence, etc., which, though fascinating, we will not explore further.)

Such a case must be contrasted with a pure accident where, for example, a doctor trips over some trailing wires and disconnects the life-support system. The baby dies before it can be reconnected. Assuming, as before, neither negligence nor carelessness on anyone's part, though the baby dies as a consequence of the doctor's actions, the doctor is not to blame because the action was involuntary (could not be helped). Interestingly, however, just because this last example was a pure accident, we should probably say that it was something that *happened* to the doctor, or in which she was involved, rather than something she did, just because there was no intention to do it.

What may we conclude from this? That if Rachels sees the distinction between active and passive euthanasia as involving the distinction between acts of omission and acts of commission, then he is quite right to insist that nothing of any moral significance turns on this distinction. If *X* allows someone to borrow her car and *deliberately* omits to tell her that the brakes do not work *with the intention* that she should crash and be killed, then that is no different in morals or in law from *X* shooting her friend (except of course that proving it might be trickier).

Suppose, however, that *X* knows that her friend's car is not properly maintained and that, sooner or later, there will be a mechanical failure. Her friend drives very fast and will probably end up killing herself. *X* foresees this and is proved right. The death of *X*'s friend is not unavoidable. *X* might have insisted that her friend repair her car and, if she did not, repaired it at her own expense. Since she did not do either of these things is she responsible for her friend's death? Few would say that she was. What does this do to the doctrine of negative responsibility? It would seem it shows it to be quite indeterminate. We probably *are* responsible for the consequences of those things *we do not do* so long as we *deliberately do not do them* with the intention of bringing about those consequences. Equally we probably *are not* responsible for the consequences of those things we *do not do* if we never dreamt and could not have known that doing them would have those consequences. Both of these positions would follow from the central place we have given intention in determining responsibility. What counts is whether we intended that what happened should have happened. What does not count, it seems, is whether we fulfil our intentions by acting positively or negatively, by act or omission.

But there is an intermediate case, and it will turn out to be an important one. If *X foresaw* the friend's accident and failed to act so as to prevent it, does she bear some responsibility (even if not entirely to blame)? She may not have *intentionally* done nothing to repair the car; but equally she did not *unintentionally* do nothing either. Suppose *X* knows that telling her friend that her car needs attention will only stiffen her friend's resolve to do nothing about it (she is like that). *X* does not intend this to be the consequence of her advice, but she foresees that it probably will be. None the less she goes ahead and says her piece. Does the fact that she has now contributed to what follows increase her responsibility? Or does the fact she still does not intend that what will follow should follow (she does not do it *in order* that . . . etc.), exonerate her still?

This problem is directly analogous to many faced by doctors (and patients and their relatives). That is, is it wrong to allow someone to die when you foresee but do not intend their death? (As we have seen with Rachels's example of Jones – pp. 138–9 above – allowing someone to die whilst intending that they should is often wrong and may be criminal.) The view that one need not be responsible for effects which are foreseen but unintended is considered in the next chapter.

NOTES

1 Foot, Philippa (1978) *Virtues and Vices*, Blackwell, p. 34.
2 Kuhse, H. and Singer, P. (1985) *Should the Baby Live?*, Oxford University Press, pp. 107–8. The source they cite is Dickeman, Mildred (1975) 'Demographic Consequences of Infanticide in Man', *Annual Review of Ecology and Systematics*, 6, pp. 121–2.
3 Plato, *Republic*, Book V, 459d–e, Paul Shorey (trans.), Loeb Classical Library, 1956 edn.
4 *Ibid.*, 461b–c.

5 Aristotle, *Politics*, Book VII, Chapter 16, 1335b, T. A. Sinclair (trans.), Penguin, 1962 edn.

6 Cited in Rachels, James (1986) *The End of Life*, Oxford University Press, p. 9.

7 See, for example, Jakobovits, I. (1959) *Jewish Medical Ethics: a Comparative and Historical Study*, Philosophical Library.

8 Central Conference of American Rabbis (1950), cited in Russell, O. Ruth (1972) *Freedom to Die: Moral and Legal Aspects of Euthanasia*, Human Sciences Press, p. 206.

9 Pope Pius XII, *The Pope Speaks*, 4, no. 4, p. 396.

10 More, Sir Thomas (1516) *Utopia*, Maurice Adams (ed.), Walter Scott Publishing Co. Ltd, London, n.d., Book II, p. 158.

11 Though Belgium, France, Germany, Holland and Italy all recognize 'mercy killing' as extenuation or as a lesser crime than murder. In 1982 the Criminal Law Review Body made a similar proposal which was not acted on. In 1976 the State of California passed a 'Natural Death Act' which permits physicians to discontinue treatment in cases of 'an incurable injury, to disease or illness' (Calif. State Assembly Bill 3060).

12 Russell, *op. cit.*, pp. 258–60.

13 *Regina* v. *Arthur* (1981), trial transcripts cited by Kuhse, H. (1984) 'A Modern Myth . . .', *Journal of Applied Philosophy*, 1, no. 1.

14 *In the Matter of Karen Quinlan, An Alleged Incompetent*, Supreme Court of New Jersey, 3 March 1976. Reprinted in Weir, Robert (ed.) (1977) *Ethical Issues in Death and Dying*, Columbia University Press, pp. 274–7.

15 *Maine Medical Center* v. *Houle*, Superior Court of the State of Maine, 14 February 1974. Reprinted in Weir, *op. cit.*, pp. 185–6.

16 See Rabkin, Gillerman and Rice (1976) 'Orders not to Resuscitate', *New England Journal of Medicine*, 292.

17 For examples, see Slater, Eliot, 'Death: the Biological Aspect', in Downing, A. B. (ed.) (1969) *Euthanasia and the Right to Death*, Peter Owen, p. 50.

18 30 August 1985.

19 See also Kuhse (1984), *op. cit.*; *The Times*, November 1981; and The Linacre Centre (1982) *Euthanasia and Clinical Practice*.

20 Cited in Braham, D. and M. (1983) 'The Arthur Case', *Journal of Medical Ethics*, vol. 9, pp. 12–15.

21 Cited in The Linacre Centre, *op.cit.*, p. 87.

22 *Ibid.*

23 Duff, R. and Campbell, A. G. M. (1983) 'Moral and Ethical Dilemmas in the Special-Care Nursery', *New England Journal of Medicine*, 289, pp. 890–4.

24 *Journal of the American Medical Association*, 227, 1974.
25 See Kuhse and Singer, *op. cit.*, pp. 11–17.
26 *Weekly Law Reports*, 1421. A short account of the similar disarray of US law on passive euthanasia may be found in Chapter 2 of Kuhse and Singer, *op. cit.*
27 Rachels, James (1975) 'Active and Passive Euthanasia', *New England Journal of Medicine*, 292, pp. 78–80; reprinted in Singer, *op. cit.*, pp. 29–35.
28 Some forms of passive euthanasia are already clearly illegal under English and US law. *Arthur* throws doubt on how extensive the prohibition is in England. For the USA, see note 26.
29 Gresham, G. A., 'A Time to be Born and a Time to Die', in Downing (ed.), *op. cit.*, p. 150.
30 The Linacre Centre, *op. cit.*, p. 57.
31 Pope Pius XII, *ibid.*
32 Though not necessary. Moral responsibility may be established by carelessness or recklessness in bringing about consequences one had a duty to avoid. See bottom of p. 139 and Chapter Seven, *passim*.
33 See *Gibbins and Proctor* (1918), 13 *Cr. App. Rep.* 134; *Pittwood* (1902), 19 TLR 37; *Bonnyman* (1942), 28 *Cr. App. Rep.* 131; *Stone and Dobinson* [1977], QB 354, [1977], 2 A11 ER 341.
34 See note 25.
35 Cited in Kuhse and Singer, *op. cit.*, p. 60.
36 Duff and Campbell, *op. cit.*, p. 892.
37 See The Linacre Centre, *op. cit.*, p. 7.
38 Church of England National Assembly (Board for Social Responsibility) (1975) *On Dying Well, An Anglican Contribution to the Debate on Euthanasia*, Church Information Office, p. 10.
39 Cited in Rachels (1986), *op. cit.*, p. 104.
40 American Medical Association, *op. cit.*, p. 728.
41 Rachels (1986), *op. cit.*, p. 93.
42 *Ibid.*, p. 94.

CHAPTER SEVEN

Extraordinary means and double effects

1 THE DOCTRINE OF DOUBLE EFFECT

A situation might arise like this: a patient is suffering from multiple complaints, some of which can be remedied by possibly painful, certainly uncomfortable, medical procedures. However, there is an underlying condition from which the patient is, in any case, going to die. The doctor decides, and the patient agrees, that these procedures should not be embarked upon. The doctor knows that this decision will probably mean that the patient's life will be shortened. Is the doctor therefore responsible for the patient's death? You can be responsible for an action you did not intend, as for example when you act negligently or without sufficient care. Is acting in the foreknowledge that what you do will cause something to happen, even if you do not, strictly, intend it, an analogous kind of case?

The *doctrine of double effect* says that, on certain conditions, you need not be responsible for those effects of your actions which, though foreseen, are not intended. It clearly matters whether or not this is a defensible view. For if the doctor in the above case were to decide that foreseeing her actions would shorten the patient's life was tantamount to intending the patient's death, or negligently risking it, then she might decide that she had no right to act that way. Alternatively, if she were convinced that causing the patient pain was an inhumane thing to do, then she might conclude that intending the patient's death was acceptable in such circumstances. As Elizabeth Anscombe puts it:

The distinction between the intended, and the merely fore-seen, effects of a voluntary action is indeed absolutely essential to Christian ethics. For Christianity forbids a number of things as being bad in themselves. But if I am answerable for the foreseen consequences of an action or refusal, as much as for the action itself, then these prohibitions will break down. If someone innocent will die unless I do a wicked thing, then on this view I am his murderer in refusing: so all that is left to me is to weigh up evils.[1]

Normally when we act, what we do is what we intended to do. Sometimes what we do is not in itself what we intend, but a means to it, as, for example, when a surgeon amputates a limb in order to save a patient's life. The surgeon does not remove the limb for the sake of it, but for a further purpose; none the less she would generally be held both to intend and to be responsible for the amputation, since it was the means whereby she accomplished what was her final intention – saving the patient. Suppose, however, a tutor tells a student that her essay is brilliant, well-constructed, tautly argued, etc. If the tutor was not caught unawares, thinking out loud or something similar, then presumably she intended what she said to her student. It is likely that the student will be pleased at these remarks, her self-confidence will be boosted and she will be flattered. Let us also suppose that this hypothetical student was not one whose confidence in any way needs boosting. Boosting her self-confidence was, indeed, the last thing that the tutor wanted to do. Nevertheless the essay *was* a brilliant, well-constructed and tautly argued piece of work, and the tutor is under a generally agreed obligation to give her students the fullest possible information about their progress and attainments. The tutor also knows that to give all that to this particular student on this particular occasion will make her insufferably bumptious and arrogant. If the tutor, knowing all this, goes ahead and tells her student the full truth about her essay, has she no excuse when her colleagues come to ask whose fault it is that the student now believes herself to be both infallible and omni-competent and is, as a consequence, almost impossible to teach?

If such decisions ought to be made on the basis of weighing

up evils, then the tutor probably does not have much of an excuse, for the possible evil of a small tactical lie about which no one need know hardly compares to the bad effects on both other tutors and other students of confirming this particular student's high opinion of herself. Equally, an obligation to weigh up consequences would make a decision to stick to the principle that this tutor owes her students the truth about their work both quixotic and selfish – in the sense that it would suggest that a personal principle was being rated more highly than the general good.

The doctrine of double effect, on the other hand, states that the tutor can remain faithful to what she sees as her contractual duty to her students without becoming responsible for the general irritations and tiresomeness which will inevitably follow. The doctrine lays down four conditions:

1 What is done must be, at the least, morally permissible.
2 What is intended must include only the good and not the bad effects of what is done.
3 The bad effects must not be the *means* whereby the good is brought about.
4 There must be *proportionality* between the good and bad effects of what is done.

Are these four conditions met in the example?

1 What was done was to give the student an assessment of her essay. That was both morally permissible and, posssibly, also required.
2 The tutor did not intend to inflate her student's ego. She intended only to give the assessment. Inflating the student's ego was something she probably would have avoided doing if she could have.
3 She did not *have* to inflate the student's ego in order to give her the assessment (as the surgeon did have to amputate the limb in order to save the patient). So inflating the student's ego was not the *means* whereby she achieved what she intended.
4 Not lying to her students about the quality of their work

is clearly a good thing in general, even were the tutor to suppose that she might choose whether to or not according to the circumstances. On the other hand, ending up with an irritating student is tiresome, but not catastrophic.

Point (4) does *not* say that the good must outweigh the bad – in this particular case it might not, as has already been noted – merely that the good and the bad must not be of entirely different orders of magnitude. For example, if a student were in such a state that to disclose her poor performance would lead her to attempt suicide, then it is scarcely proper even to try to weigh the good of fulfilling one's contractual duties against the risk of the loss of a life. This is, perhaps, a little strained as an example, since tutors seldom face such extreme dilemmas. Doctors often do, however.

It may be felt that this last point exposes a weakness in the doctrine, namely the vagueness of the idea of 'proportionality'. In what kind of cases, *exactly*, is one permitted to weigh good and evil consequences against one another in deciding what to do (and thereby, of course, to adopt something like a utilitarian calculus)? This is not the only vagueness here, either. The distinction between means and ends is not always clear. Jonathan Bennett quotes the following example:

> The following kind of thing can occur. A woman in labour will certainly die unless an operation is performed in which the head of her unborn child is crushed or dissected; while if it is not performed the child can be delivered, alive, by post-mortem caesarean section.[2]

Classically, the doctrine of double effect, as interpreted by Roman Catholic moralists, would permit allowing the mother to die, but would not permit killing the child in order to save the mother. Allowing the mother to die, assuming it is not intended, is permitted because it is not the *means* by which the child's life is saved, nor is it worse than killing the child would be. Killing the child, on the other hand, would be an intentional killing since, if we intend to save the mother's life, we must kill the child in order to do so. This interpretation of the doctrine is troublesome, not merely because for most non-Catholics (and, perhaps, for many Roman Catholics too) it yields a highly counter-intuitive result. It also rests on the unexamined assumption that saving the child is permissible because allowing the woman to die is permissible, whereas saving the woman is impermissible because killing the child is impermissible. Since the question just *is* whether allowing the woman to die is permissible whereas killing the child is not, this seems to beg the question from the beginning (see condition (1) of the doctrine, p. 155 above). It also seems questionable whether it is clear that killing the child *is* a means to saving the woman whereas allowing the woman to die is *not* a means to saving the child. It has been suggested[3] that killing the child is *not* the means by which the woman would be saved. She is saved by having the child removed from her womb. Though the child will not survive removal from the womb (because in order to be removed, the surgeon must 'alter [its] . . . dimensions in certain ways',[4] i.e. crush its head), its death is not the means by which the mother is saved.

Whether this is convincing does not matter for an exactly parallel uncertainty affects the question of whether the mother's death is a means to saving the child's life. A caesarean section cannot be performed while the mother is still alive, for the child's head is already in the birth canal. Only after the mother is dead, therefore, can we save the child, and in that sense we need the mother to die if the child's life is to be saved. Does that make the mother's death the *means* we employ to save the child?

This example has been used to cast doubt on the validity of the doctrine of double effect (by Bennett, amongst others), but it is not clear that it does, unless it is assumed that the doctrine yields a clear answer in this case. The point about the case is not that the doctrine gives us an indefensible answer, as many have supposed, but that it does not give a clear answer at all. Look at the four conditions again:

1   *Is the action morally permissible?* Since the doctrine requires an answer to this, it does not itself provide one, it is not an

objection to the *doctrine* if we do not know what the answer is. Certainly Roman Catholic commentators have assumed that allowing the woman to die is permissible, whereas killing the child is not, but this is an assumption commonly brought to the doctrine, not a consequence of the doctrine itself. We have seen that it is unlikely that the bare difference between killing and letting die, *in itself*, decides the issue one way or the other.

2   *Are only the good effects of the action directly intended?* If we save the woman, do we intend the death of the child; or if we save the child, do we intend the death of the woman? We may suppose that the surgeon would want neither the woman nor the child to die, if that were possible. So either way the death is not directly intended. But we are generally held to intend not just our ends, but also the means whereby we attain those ends (see above, p. 154), so this question will be answered by the answer to the next one.

3   *Are the bad effects of the action the means whereby the good effects are brought about?* This, as we have seen, is unclear (see above, p. 157). In either alternative there are good but inconclusive reasons for seeing the death of one as the means whereby the life of the other is saved.

4   *Are the good and the bad effects of what is intended proportional?* Those who would see all human life as equally valuable must see the effects, in either case, as equally balanced, since it is a life for a life, either way. However, Don Locke points out that many would see the unborn child as not having 'the same moral rights and status as an adult human being'.[5] This difference may itself account for our different moral intuitions about how the case should be decided; in any event, the answer to this question will turn on one's attitude to the value of infant as compared with adult life.

In this case, then, conditions (2) and (3) are not clearly met, and (1) and (4) may or may not be met according to one's prior moral beliefs. For most of us, in all likelihood, our moral intuitions about (1) and (4) will be unclear. The reason why the doctrine gives us a clear and probably uncontested answer in the case of the student, and fails to do so in the case of the woman and child, is therefore to be found in the different moral intuitions we feed into the doctrine, not in a failure in the doctrine itself. For the doctrine is not a theory about what is right and wrong, but an attempt to formalize our intuitions about the rightness and wrongness of particular cases. It does not tell us whether certain actions are right or wrong; it tells us whether performing them makes us responsible for certain foreseen consequences that may follow from performing them. Thus disagreement about whether the doctrine has given us an acceptable result can largely be traced back to prior disagreement about whether it was right or wrong to perform the actions in the first place. For example, the doctrine says that, in abiding by her general duties to her students, a tutor need not be responsible for the troublesome consequences of so doing. It does not say that the tutor must regard those duties as overriding any other duties she may feel she has. It says that a doctor, in administering drugs to a patient which may shorten that patient's life, is not responsible for that patient's death if her intention was to relieve pain and not to shorten life. The doctrine does *not* say that a doctor must relieve pain, or that killing is always wrong and forbidden.

So all this does *not* tell us whether declining to treat a patient is ever permissible – a question to which we clearly still need an answer.

2 EXTRAORDINARY MEANS

In the attempt to answer this question, particularly in situations where the wisdom of continued treatment may be doubted, moralists have distinguished between *extraordinary* and *ordinary* means of treatment. A doctor is held, according to this distinction, to be bound to adopt ordinary means of treatment but may choose, with the patient's consent if available, to discontinue extraordinary means. This distinction, if it is well-founded, would determine in which cases it was permissible to cease to treat. (And for Roman

Catholics, who are forbidden suicide, it determines which treatments a patient may justifiably decline.)

Like the doctrine of double effect, the distinction between ordinary and extraordinary means of treatment has had a very bad press in the recent philosophical literature.[6] The main objections to it are that it is vague, relative and smuggles in judgements about the expected quality of a life whilst at the same time purporting not to use them as the basis for life and death decisions. Since the distinction in practice, it is alleged, seems to categorize as 'ordinary' those treatments which would improve the quality of life of the patient, and as 'extraordinary' those which stand little or no chance of doing so, then why not simply abandon the whole apparatus of double effect and extraordinary means altogether? The question of whether to opt for life or death for the patient might then be confronted directly and clearly and decided on a rational determination of the likely consequences.

This objection, if justified, is a grave one, for the whole point of appeals to the doctrine of double effect and the ordinary/extraordinary distinction is to support the belief that death may be a forseeable result of a permissible action without its being thereby true that death has been chosen as the intended outcome. If all sorts of practices which most people would find entirely morally defensible and humane are actually cases of intentionally choosing death – i.e. cases of killing – then we must either give them up, or else admit that killing people is permissible in a much wider range of cases than we currently believe it to be.

The first point to note is that many critics of the ordinary/extraordinary distinction are, in one respect, pushing at an open door. The distinction is not meant to characterize different kinds of treatment on medical grounds alone; nor was it ever meant to yield a clear list of prescribed and optional treatments. Many of its strongest advocates see it as a normative distinction, made relative to different situations:

> . . . according to circumstances of persons, places, times and culture [ordinary means are] . . . means that do not involve any grave burden for oneself or another.[7]

Past moralists used the term *ordinary means for saving life* as an ethical category; it *meant* imperative. They used the term *extraordinary means* as one of moral permission; it *meant* electable or morally dispensable means.[8]

Seen in this light it becomes clear why the very same treatment can be ordinary for one patient in one set of circumstances and extraordinary for another patient in different circumstances. It also needs to be borne in mind that the ordinary/extraordinary distinction is meant to operate in conjunction with the doctrine of double effect. From this it follows that what would otherwise be extraordinary means must be required treatment (and therefore 'ordinary') if the only possible intention in not employing them was to bring about the death of the patient, and doing that is forbidden. In other words, as traditionally employed, the ordinary/extraordinary distinction does involve quality of life judgements, but killing the patient (or declining to treat with the intention that she should die) need not be considered as one of the options available. To see what this means, consider these two examples:

1 An elderly patient was diagnosed as having acute myeloblastic monocytic leukaemia, which is inevitably fatal. Chemotherapy can bring about a temporary remission of between two and thirteen months in about thirty to fifty per cent of cases, but the results are poorer for elderly patients and there are often serious side effects. It was decided not to treat the patient with chemotherapy.[9]

2 A Down's syndrome baby suffered from a duodenal obstruction which required surgery without which it could not take nourishment and would die. It was decided to operate.[10]

In (1) a course of chemotherapy can be considered 'extraordinary' because the prospects of a remission were poor, the burden of the treatment great and the patient terminally ill. For other cancers and other patients chemotherapy could well be a standard, and an 'ordinary', course of treatment. In declining to adopt a course of chemotherapy the doctor was not opting for the death of the patient, since that was inevitable anyway (or as inevitable as any medical prognosis can indicate). The decision that had to be taken concerned only the quality of the patient's remaining life. It did not, and could not, encompass the question of whether it would be better for the patient to have any life remaining to him at all. Declining to continue chemotherapy would not, therefore, count as killing on the doctor's part, nor as suicide on the part of the patient.

In (2) on the other hand, declining to operate on the baby would be choosing death for it, since its condition was not, given current medical knowledge and skill, fatal. Thus whether we decided that the treatment was usual or unusual, we could not claim that in declining it, we were not aiming at the baby's death. Some may argue that because of the Down's syndrome, the baby would be better off dead. But even if that were conceded, it would not follow that not treating it for its intestinal obstruction was merely to 'allow it to die'. The doctrine of double effect shows that in such a case, because the treatment is 'ordinary' (i.e. required, mandatory), non-treatment would have to amount to intentional killing. Whether *that* was justified would depend on one's view about the moral status and rights of newborn babies, and the relative strictness of the prohibition on intentional killing. What it would *not* depend on is whether it was killed by not treating the immediately life-threatening condition or by some other method.

We are not, therefore, always responsible for the foreseen consequences of our actions or omissions. In particular, acting under the guidance of a justifiable moral principle can be a complete defence to the charge that we knowingly brought about some evil consequence.

3 GROUNDS FOR EUTHANASIA

In Chapter Six we saw that in many cases Rachels is right, there is no moral difference between killing and letting die. Advocates of passive euthanasia need not be, and many clearly are not, committed to the view that there is a moral difference. Some are probably committed to the view that in some cases killing a patient is a perfectly proper thing to do. These advocate passive euthanasia only because they believe active euthanasia to be prohibited by law, whereas passive euthanasia is permitted. (This may be doubted – see p. 131 above, and associated note 26.)

In this chapter we have outlined a view which is more complicated than the one that Rachels attacks and therefore is not susceptible to the criticisms that he raises. Those who hold this view do not believe that passive euthanasia is merely a matter of not saving the life of someone whose life you could have saved. They believe that in cases where the patient's death is imminent or where treatment is painful and offers only a very remote chance of success then it is justifiable, if the patient and/or her relatives consent, to cease to attempt to save the patient's life. But they also accept that this leaves them with an obligation to continue to offer treatments and procedures which will, while they cannot save life and may even shorten it, make the process of dying as acceptable as possible to the patient and her relatives.

To take this course is not to kill the patient; it is to allow her to die. Allowing something to happen can be done through action or inaction. I can allow a valuable vase to fall to the floor and break by not trying to catch it, or by moving out of its way when it threatens to fall into my arms.[11] So allowing someone to die can be done actively or passively. Whether it amounts to, or is as bad as, killing them depends on whether one acted or failed to act *with the intention that* they should die. If their death was merely foreseen as a consequence of doing something which was itself wholly permissible, and was not intended either as a means or as an end, then not saving them was not killing them.

Moral responsibility for an event is not determined by whether it came about because one acted, or because one failed to act. Acting does not necessarily make one responsible, and not acting does not necessarily absolve one from responsibility. Rather moral responsibility is determined by one's intentions and duties. If someone is stabbed in the street and taken to a hospital where, because a doctor declines to treat her for the stab wounds, she dies, then both the assailant and the doctor carry moral responsibility for her death. The assailant is responsible because she intended, or was prepared to risk, her victim's death. The doctor is responsible because she violated a duty of care to her patient in a grossly negligent way. Consequently, though both are responsible, they are guilty of different things: the assailant of murder, and the doctor of criminal negligence. The doctor's negligence could amount to murder if the patient was neglected *in order that* she should die. This would be a special, and rather unusual case (though see *Bonnyman*, p. 122 above).

But a doctor only has a strict duty to use ordinary means. Declining to adopt measures with little or no prospect of success and which additionally involve risk, .hardship or disproportionate pain for the patient, is perfectly justifiable. One may not, therefore, hold the doctor responsible if the patient dies when she might, if treated, have lived a little longer. It is only in this sense that 'letting a patient die' is clearly morally acceptable.

It does not follow that euthanasia may not be justifiable on other grounds, though it does follow that it can never be justified merely on the grounds that it is passive, omitting to act rather than directly killing. For the sake of completeness we will indicate what those grounds may be, though strictly it lies outside the remit of this chapter to discuss them in the detail they deserve.

There is a legal right to refuse treatment. Competent patients – those adults of sound mind who have understood the facts of their case – may decline to be treated. This is at least consistent with the fact that there are no legal sanctions on suicide, since to decline life-saving treatment may be thought a kind of suicide. Nor should the fact that they choose to decline life-saving treatment be thought in itself to cast doubt on their competency, for if there are quasi-rational grounds for committing suicide, then declining treatment is not of necessity an irrational thing to do. It is one thing to disagree with someone about the wisdom, or even the morality, of refusing treatment, it is another to override their autonomy and treat them against their will. Allowing a patient to die in such circumstances may or may not properly be termed 'euthanasia', but it is hard to see that it is forbidden, given what that would entail. It sometimes happens that Jehovah's Witnesses refuse blood transfusions in circumstances where their death will result from that refusal.[12] Is it a worse thing to let them die, which they are clearly prepared to do, than to override their belief in something which is, for them, of paramount importance? It does not seem obvious that it is.

But a patient who has a right to decline treatment does not thereby have a right to ask for further assistance where simply stopping treatment will not be enough to bring about her death. Nor, probably, does a doctor or a nurse have the right to offer such assistance or to accede to requests for it, unless doing so is justified on grounds other than the patient's wish to die. To say that they might do so would make it too easy for crimes to shelter under spurious defences. It is also true that whereas someone has a perfect right to harm herself, no one has a right to harm her just because she asks to be harmed, even if she does.

But there may well be extreme cases where the suffering of the patient is so great and, because of the circumstances, no remedy for it exists, that killing the patient is the only means available to prevent the pain. This may happen in sudden emergencies or in war, or in parts of the world where extremely limited or no medical resources are available.[13] We would not wish to say that in such a case active euthanasia would be wrong.

Finally, there are the cases which figure so prominently in the literature, of deformed or disabled infants who are born with little or no prospect of a life free from pain, from the burden of repeated surgical intervention and from gross handicap. Many of these will be cases that fall into categories already discussed since often it will be a matter of deciding whether, and for how long, to fend off their death, rather than deciding whether they should live. But some do not suffer from conditions which threaten their lives or, if they do, those conditions can be remedied to the extent where they can, at least, expect to live for a significant period.

Down's syndrome children, as we have seen, are often born with a duodenal obstruction which can normally be corrected by surgery and which, in an otherwise healthy child, would be so treated. There is no case for allowing most of these children to die of the uncorrected obstruction since they will be capable of lives at least as happy and satisfying as most of us manage. It may be that we cannot ask those parents who are unable or unwilling to shoulder the immense burden of care and attention such children need, to do so. But if so, we should provide what facilities are necessary, not remove the demand for them by allowing the children to die. Otherwise we seem to have granted that those individuals, who in order to live moderately well, will demand more resources from the rest of us than they are able to provide in return, can be killed in order to save us the burden of supplying those needs. How many of us could survive such a test, stringently applied?[14]

Spina bifida children pose more difficult problems. Some of them can be treated moderately successfully but some, if treated at all, will require extremely burdensome, painful and frequent treatment and even then will face a chronically miserable life.[15] Though these latter cases probably would not fall under the double effect and extraordinary treatment tests, none the less it seems inhumane to prolong such suffering when it might have been ended shortly after birth. Despite the campaigns of organizations like LIFE and the Society for the Protection of the Unborn Child, it would seem to be generally believed that unborn fœtuses do not have the same rights to life as adults do. It does not follow from this that abortion is morally totally justified but that, even if it is not, it is not as serious a crime as the murder or manslaughter of an adult or child. (See Don Locke's remark in (4) on p. 158 above.) Thus, though we would not kill an adult or grown child who suffered such disabilities and handicaps as have been described, there might be less compelling reasons for not killing a young baby soon after birth. In any event, the Down's syndrome example (above) shows that discussion of this problem must turn on the interests of the child itself, and not on any weighing up of costs and benefits to others.

Much of the strength and plausibility of the case for euthanasia lies in the alleged fact that it is something we always accept as morally justifiable and which is, and always has been, practised. Thus many cases of humanely ceasing to offer life-preserving treatment, or of refusing unnecessarily to prolong the process of dying, are cited in support of this case.

We have shown, we believe, that the most defensible and intuitively acceptable of these cases are not instances of euthanasia at all. With the qualifications we have discussed, not treating or otherwise failing to save life in such cases does not amount to killing or its moral equivalent. Such cases do not, therefore, lend support to the view that killing a human being may sometimes be morally justifiable.

It may be possible to make a case for voluntary euthanasia in extreme cases and where the answer to the question 'Is it for the sake of the patient that death is being considered?' is 'yes'. That cannot be ruled out. But if we were always to alleviate pain as successfully as technically we are now able, and if we were to do as much to compensate for the effects of disabilities and handicaps as we might, then the necessity for that question to be asked would be much less great than it presently is.

Killing someone, in some circumstances, may well be the least bad of the available alternatives. It does not follow that it is ever morally desirable.

NOTES

1 Anscombe, G. E. M., 'War and Murder', in her (1981) *Collected Philosophical Papers*, vol. III, Blackwell, p. 58.
2 Bennett, J. (1966) 'Whatever the Consequences', *Analysis*, 26, p. 83.
3 Geddes, L. (1973) 'On the Intrinsic Wrongness of Killing Innocent People', *Analysis*, 33, p. 94.
4 *Ibid.*
5 Locke, D. (1982) 'The Choice Between Lives', *Philosophy*, 57, p. 456.
6 Rachels, Harris, Glover and Kuhse and Singer all reject it as a useful distinction. See Rachels (1986), *op. cit.*, pp. 96–100; Harris, J. (1985) *The Value of Life*, Routledge & Kegan Paul, p. 39; Kuhse and Singer, *op. cit.*, pp. 30–7; Glover, *op. cit.*, pp. 195–7.
7 Pope Pius XII, *op. cit.*, p. 396.

8 Ramsey, Paul (1978) *Ethics at the Edges of Life*, Yale University Press, p. 153.

9 This is an edited version of case no. 18 in Beauchamp, T. L. and Childress, J. F. (1983, 2nd edn) *Principles of Biomedical Ethics*, Oxford University Press, p. 305.

10 Based on case no. 17 in Beauchamp, T. L. and Childress, J. F. (1979) *Principles of Biomedical Ethics*, pp. 266–7.

11 A full discussion of this point appears in Locke, *op. cit.*, pp. 463–4. This whole section is much indebted to the arguments that appear there.

12 See Beauchamp and Childress (1983), *op. cit.*, case nos 13 and 14.

13 See Church of England National Assembly, *op. cit.*, p. 10.

14 This may be an argument against some abortions. See Hursthouse, R. (1987) *Beginning Lives*, Blackwell, *passim*. But *cf.* below (p. 166) and Locke (1982), *op. cit.*

15 See for example case no. 19 in Beauchamp and Childress (1979), *op. cit.*, pp. 268–9.

CHAPTER EIGHT

Should the numbers count?

1 THE ETHICS OF RESOURCE ALLOCATION

In 1948 when the National Health Service was set up in the UK, it was funded on the assumption that demand for its services would actually go down as people got healthier. This has not happened. Virtually all state-financed welfare schemes are chronically under-resourced and over-stretched, and this was true even before the world-wide financial squeeze of the late 'seventies and 'eighties. The peculiar logic of state welfare schemes seems to mean that they fuel the felt needs they are designed to eliminate. Kenneth Boyd, a research fellow with the Edinburgh Medical Group, wrote in 1979:

> Advances in medicine and improved living standards have ensured that more people now live longer and healthier lives: but they have also heightened popular expectations of health and made continued medical progress a presupposition of public opinion . . .
> Despite escalating public and private expenditure on health care, demand progressively outpaces supply . . . the problem is not simply one of an immediate economic recession, but in one way or another it is endemic to the health care systems of all Western countries.[1]

So it seems that unless we could realistically envisage a future in which finite demand were matched by indefinitely large resources, there will always be a problem about how available resources should be distributed amongst those who have a claim on them. For not all of those claims could ever be met in full.

The problem is exemplified in the kind of dilemma we are familiar with where the demands of the chronically ill – those in need of hip replacement surgery, for example – have to be matched against the treatment of acute need, e.g. renal (kidney) failure. The difficulty is most pointed where we are faced with life and death decisions. Until quite recently, a priority was placed on the creation of acute coronary care units. These were equipped with special apparatus for the resuscitation of patients suffering from myocardial infarctions (coronary heart failure). It quite soon became apparent, however, that this strategy created more problems than it solved for it resulted in an increase in patients with an acute need for treatment. The physiological state which had led to the heart attack itself was not alleviated by the coronary care unit, but remained to be dealt with. Ironically, of course, prior to the introduction of the units, many of these patients would have died and, therefore, made no further demands on the health services.

Coronary care units were, in Boyd's phrase 'expensive mistakes'.[2] They did exactly what they had been intended to do – preserved the lives of acutely ill patients who would otherwise have died. That the state would thereby be burdened with patients who were still acutely ill and in need of further care and treatment had not been allowed for. The efficiency of the procedures adopted led to a need to spend even more money.

The treatment of chronic coronary heart disease raises further problems. One of its symptoms is angina – pain, sometimes severe and occasionally totally disabling, which can spread through the whole of the upper body. Coronary bypass surgery will often relieve the angina, but at a cost of £6000 per operation and with no significant increase in the patient's life expectancy. It seems more than likely that many of the things which make coronary heart disease one of the West's most significant single causes of early death can be altered. Important causal factors appear to be family history, diet and smoking. Clearly something can be done about these last two and arguably if the money spent in the last

twenty years on coronary care had been spent instead on
effective health education campaigns designed to inform the
lay public about the real dangers of high fat diets and
cigarettes, then more lives could have been saved than have
been. Coronary heart disease cannot be cured; at best the
damage it inflicts can be repaired, but without a change in
life-style the patient's prognosis is poor. The condition can
be prevented in those cases where it is not entirely due to
constitutional genetic factors.

This is a particular case of a more general principle which
is being increasingly urged: that preventive medicine will in
fact do more to improve the nation's health than our current
emphasis on acute care, on a cost for cost basis. The 'Black
Report' on *Inequalities in Health* (1980) argues strongly for a
shift of resources away from acute care towards a rectification
of those material and social inequalities which, it suggests,
are largely responsible for much of the ill-health that health
services are presently struggling to treat.

It seems at least likely that this could be true. If it is,
however, it is important to see what its costs would be as
well as its benefits. Just as, if the 'Black Report' is right,
there are many who will die, who might have been saved
by a switch to preventive medicine, so there are many who
will now be saved who would not be if the Report's
recommendations were accepted.

> . . . heart transplants, often cited as an example of expensive
> and wasteful medicine, may not be a solution to heart disease,
> but equally heart disease that has not been prevented will
> continue to exist even in the best regulated society.[3]

But if the expensive high-technology units necessary for
heart transplants were discontinued in order to fund a
programme of preventive care, many of the people who still
need heart transplant operations would not be able to obtain
them.

This is not a criticism of the conclusions in the 'Black
Report', but a general observation about the problems
inherent in any pattern of resource allocation for health care.
Any decision about distribution which falls short of giving
everyone as much as they need will imply that some are to

be denied in order to benefit others. The question is not whether this is acceptable, since it would seem to be unavoidable, but rather on what basis such decisions are to be made.

The issues at stake here can be illustrated by what has come to be called the Scarce Drug problem.[4] We have available a limited quantity of some drug which is sufficient to save the life of one seriously-ill patient. There are five other patients, however, who will also die unless treated, but their illnesses are not so far advanced. Each of the five could be saved, therefore, by one-fifth of the total available.

To whom do we give the drug? It cannot be shared out on an equal basis, for then each would get one-sixth of the total. This is not enough to save any of them, and so all would die. We have to choose between treating the one who needs all of the drug, or treating the five who each need a fifth. An apparently rational solution to this problem would be to choose that course of action which saved the most lives; to give the drug to the five, in other words. It would have to be conceded that this would mean, regrettably, that the one could not be saved, but then it would be all the more regrettable if the five could not be.

This solution to the Scarce Drug problem is based on the principle of maximizing the numbers of lives saved. It seems an eminently defensible one for allocating scarce medical resources and is one of the planks on which the 'Black Report' conclusions rest. If human life is valuable, then clearly more human life is more valuable than less, other things being equal.

The principle also has an air of commonsense reality about it, and the virtue of a quantifiable criterion. We may surely measure the effectiveness of different kinds of treatments or different health policies in terms of numbers of lives saved. Where evidence of that kind is not available it should be sought out. It would be grossly irresponsible to treat patients in a particular way and then not seek to determine whether they lived or died as a consequence. This evidence would then be used to show where the limited resources available actually did most good in terms of lives saved. For example:

Action	Cost per Life Saved
Rebuilding Tower Blocks to improved standards after Ronan Point disaster.	£64 million
Implementing improved Fire Regulations in NHS hospitals.	£12 million
Fitting crash barriers to all major UK roads.	£117,000
Fitting roofs on tractor cabs.	£250,000
Maintaining sufficient kidney dialysis machines to treat all in need.	£4400
Fitting child-proof lids on all drug containers.	£3000[5]

The principle of maximizing the benefits in terms of lives saved would imply that we should work through such lists as this, allocating money first where the cost is least, and last, if any money remains, where the cost is highest. The attraction of such a policy is obvious:

> [Physician]: 'You can't get away from it – if it can't be measured, then it's not important, and you can't take it into account in decision-making.'[6]

Yet even as a crude first measure, numbers of lives saved per alternative policy is not as helpful as it may seem. We cannot simply count the numbers of people who have died, for, after all, some of them would have died anyway. In a sense, life is never saved; death is merely postponed a little longer. That in turn suggests that it is not numbers of lives we must count, but years of life, and that instantly complicates the equation. It is, furthermore, hard to resist the idea that quality of life must count as well. A surgical procedure may stop people dying, but if it leaves them severely disabled, unconscious or semi-conscious, or in continuous severe pain, is it worth carrying out?

A further problem is that the maximizing policy carries

unexpected and probably unwelcome commitments. If a policy is to maximize the total amount of pain-free and worthwhile life, then we are committed not just to saving life whenever we can. Perhaps a greater pay off in terms of maximization might come from abandoning the treatment of the sick and damaged and concentrating all our efforts and resources into producing as many babies as possible. If all women of child-bearing age were pregnant as often as possible, and a certain minimum of resources went into ante-natal care and immunization programmes, then we might maximize the total amount of human life on the planet more successfully than in any other way.[7]

Much more could be said about the problems of the maximization principle but for the present the crucial point is that such a policy carries a commitment to sacrificing the welfare and the rights of those currently alive and in need, in favour of those not yet born, or even conceived. This is solely on the basis that, potentially, there are more of the latter than the former.

Our favoured solution to the Scarce Drug problem – saving the five, and letting the one die – may still be the right solution, but we should feel increasingly that the maximization principle, by itself, is not an adequate explanation of why our favoured solution is the best one. Certainly, the principle fares less well when faced with more complicated examples. Elizabeth Anscombe has argued that in the Scarce Drug problem we do the five no wrong if we choose to treat the one.[8] This may seem a bizarre suggestion in the context of the problem as it was outlined above (p. 172), but in slightly different situations it no longer looks so odd, as we shall see.

Suppose the drug we are about to administer to the individual who needs it actually belongs to her. It is a very expensive extract of a very rare plant and she and her friends have expended a great deal of money and effort in locating a supply and raising the money to pay for it. Is it still so very obvious that the right thing to say is, 'I'm sorry, but five people in the next ward could be saved by just the dose necessary to save you alone, so we are going to take it from you and give it to them'? We may feel that she has some sort of obligation in charity to consider doing the noble thing and donating the drug to the five in the next ward, but few would argue that we have the right to take it from her at the cost of her own life. Oddly enough, this seems to follow even if not at the cost of a life. In Pittsburgh in 1978 a man died of aplastic anaemia after an unsuccessful attempt to persuade his cousin, the only known compatible donor, to donate the twenty-one ounces of bone marrow he needed to survive. US law said that he did not have the right to compel his cousin to donate the bone marrow.[9] However monstrous the cousin's behaviour might be, given that donating the bone marrow posed no threat to him at all, it would be equally monstrous to remove twenty-one ounces of someone's bone marrow without their consent and against their wishes.

2   NUMBERS

I am walking by the sea and notice someone stranded on a rock by the incoming tide. At the quayside there is a rowing boat and I have, without putting myself at any undue risk, just about time to reach the rock before the tide covers it. Just as I am about to cast off, I notice another rock on which two people are stranded, also by the rising tide. It is clear that there is not time to reach both rocks and save all three people, and given that I have already accepted some kind of obligation to render assistance, it seems obvious that I ought to row to the rock with two on it, rather than to the other which has only one.[10]

Just as in the first version of the Scarce Drug problem, where the issue of who owned the drug was not raised (p. 172 above), so here the morality of saving the two rather than the one seems clear. Equally, the explanation seems to be that the principle of maximization demands that we choose that option which saves the most lives. We must choose between saving one and saving two. We do not know anything about any of them, except that they will die if not rescued. So the only thing which differentiates the various alternative courses of action open to me is the numbers. If I go home and have tea, then three will die. If I row to the rock with only one person on it, then two will die. If I row to the rock with two on it, then only one will die.

In a straight choice between saving one and saving two it seems clear that we must save two. It is not clear that we may save two at the cost of killing one, rather than just not saving one. Bernard Williams has given a famous example of this kind:

> Jim finds himself in the central square of a small South American town. Tied up against the wall are a row of twenty Indians, most terrified, a few defiant, in front of them several armed men in uniform. The Captain in charge . . . explains that the Indians are a random group of inhabitants who, after recent protests against the government, are just about to be killed to remind other possible protesters of the advantages of not protesting. However, since Jim is an honoured visitor . . . the Captain is happy to offer him a guest's privilege of killing one of the Indians himself. If Jim accepts, then as a special mark of the occasion, the other Indians will be let off. Of course, if Jim refuses, then there is no special occasion and Pedro here will do what he was about to do when Jim arrived, and kill them all.[11]

This is, of course, a hard case, it was designed that way. The point is not what advice should be offered to Jim – in such a desperate and horrific situation in reality advice would be impertinent. The real point is that if the maximization principle applied generally, then this would not be a hard case at all. If the mark of the correct decision in the rowing boat case and the first version of the Scarce Drug problem is that more lives are saved than lost, then how much more obvious should it be that the right decision in this case is the one which saves nineteen lives rather than none? (We may assume, and Williams goes to some lengths to ensure, that there is no realistic third choice: either shoot one and save nineteen, or decline the offer and know that all twenty will be shot. We may also assume that there will be no further consequences that will affect the final count of lives saved versus lives lost.)

The difficulty, and the awful fascination, of the case can

be set aside for the moment. An advocate of the maximization principle might argue that the solution *is* clear, and that only moral conservatism, squeamishness or hypocrisy prevents us from seeing it as clear. It may be, in the end, that the solution is the one that the maximizer is urging on us, and that what Jim should do is to shoot one of the Indians. (The Indians themselves are begging Jim to do just that, so their consent is not an obstacle to his doing it.) Let us, therefore, grant that the maximization principle is applicable here, for the sake of the argument, and see where it leads.

We should notice that, if the maximization principle is correct, then the fact that the rowing boat and Scarce Drug example do not involve killing anyone, whereas the Indians' case does, is of no moral significance. In other words, the maximization principle's solution to the Indians' case implies that killing someone and not saving their life are morally equivalent. We have already, in Chapter Six, met this suggestion and we granted there that it does seem to be true in some circumstances. Is it true in these cases?

Most people's reactions to these cases suggest very strongly that they do not think it is. If Jim's predicament caused you any hesitation at all, then it must have been because Jim must kill in order to save life, for if it were a simple choice between saving nineteen and saving none, there would be no problem.

But for the advocate of the maximization principle there should be no hesitation. Since the principle is concerned only with numbers of lives saved, and not with how they come to be saved, it does not matter whether lives are saved by averting threats to life, or by refraining from taking life, or by taking life in order to avert threats. As long as the overall balance of lives saved versus lives lost comes out in credit rather than debit, then the right alternative has been chosen.

If the maximization principle is fully accepted in the uncomplicated version sketched in the last paragraph, then the way is opened for what has been called 'utilitarian planning carried to a new extreme'.[12]

John Harris's 'The Survival Lottery'[13] proposes that in a future in which organ transplants had been perfected to the point where they threatened no greater risk than any other surgical intervention, it would be morally obligatory to adopt the Survival Lottery. Under this scheme donors, selected at random, would be killed in order to redistribute their healthy organs amongst those who would die without them. One healthy donor might in this way save the lives of two patients with acute renal failure, one with liver failure and one who has chronic cardiac problems with a need for heart–lung surgery. This apparently repugnant suggestion has more going for it than it might at first seem. A doctor has an obligation to save life. This is the same obligation that we all have; doctors just have greater opportunities to satisfy it than most of us. It therefore follows that a doctor has an obligation to do whatever is necessary to save her patients from dying. If organ transplants will save their lives, then organ transplants must be carried out. If dead donors are neither available nor suitable, then the doctor must take the organs from live donors, or else let her patients die. It does, of course, mean that the donor will die. If the donor is not killed in order to free her organs, then the patient will die. If there are more patients than donors, then killing the donor(s) will save more lives than are lost. According to the maximization principle, the right course of action to choose is that which results in saving more lives than are lost. So according to the maximization principle the right thing to do is to kill the donor in order to free her organs and save lives that would otherwise be lost. We have seen that for the principle it does not matter *how* lives are saved or lost, so long as more lives are saved than are lost. The Survival Lottery is not only entirely consistent with the maximization principle, therefore, it is actually a logical consequence of it.

If this is accepted then a little tidying up of loose ends is all that is required. The donor has to be chosen by lottery to avoid unfairly victimizing some individual or group within the population. The benefits of the lottery are a virtual guarantee that no one will die of organ failure so that the risks of being called on to be a donor are heavily outweighed by the likelihood of having one's life saved by a successful organ transplant. No one with self-induced illness or damage is to be eligible so that the natural incentive for individuals to keep themselves as fit and healthy as possible is not reduced. So long as each donor's death ensures that at least two lives are saved that would otherwise be lost, then everyone stands a better chance of surviving in the lottery than outside it.

The simultaneous appeal to altruism and self-interest made by the Survival Lottery is a powerful one. It is therefore all the more curious that hardly anyone accepts it as a serious socio-political ideal. Most, indeed, find it morally repellent. Sometimes this repugnance is expressed in terms of a distaste for taking moral decisions on the basis of numbers. There is something in this, but probably not as much as it first seems. We do value right action spontaneously and uncalculatingly undertaken, despite the admonishments of some moral philosophers who would accept reason alone as a proper ground for moral judgements. Up to a point a sound intuition underlies the preference for spontaneous moral judgements. All else being equal, someone who instinctively knows the right thing to do is more help to us than someone who insists on reasoning it out, for the situation is probably being made worse by the time she is taking to do so.

We also know that it is an illusion that someone who can make quick decisions authoritatively can also make the right decisions. We would like to feel that such people exist, but we know that instinctive judgements are as often wrong as right. Moral decisions based on numbers may be distasteful to us to the extent that they show a reflective rather than an instinctive approach to ethics, but it would be foolish to reject the appeal to numbers on that account.

A second objection is that the appeal to numbers is necessarily detached and impersonal. Relationships between friends, on the other hand, often depend on a kind of loyalty which is partial and interested. Many would value that loyalty as a more truly human motive for choices and actions, above the calculations which treat everyone alike as interchangeable units. But to value the kind of consideration which *should* weigh with friends from those who occupy roles as policy-makers and decision-takers is short-sighted since it merely flatters us without genuinely advancing our

interests. 'If ever I had to choose between betraying my
friend and betraying my country,' E. M. Forster once
notoriously said, 'I hope I should have the courage to betray
my country.' If we are impressed by this, then we are
thinking of the times when the country has got it wrong.
We are also probably thinking of the government rather
than the country, of the apparatus of power and vested
interest rather than the people as a whole. It is far less
impressive once one considers how it would be for those
who, innocently, *are* the country, but are not amongst
Forster's friends. The Mafia is an organization which places
the interests of its friends above those of the rest of us. It
often puts itself forward as embodying no more than the
old code of honour and loyalty. But it is precisely because
it embodies those values and precious few others that it is
so objectionable.

Certainly arguments which turn on numbers can be
abused. We often, quite rightly, have the feeling that such
arguments too easily become solely arithmetical and lose
sight of those dimensions of the problem which are not
easily quantified. We may also, in arguing about numbers,
run the risk of forgetting what those numbers stand for.
Often it seems that arguments about levels and rates of
unemployment fall into both traps. The issue of how the
statistics are collected and how they are to be added up gain
prominence over discussion of ways of remedying the
problem. Debating points scored in disputing methodologies
and evidence obscure the reality of what it means to be
unemployed and why it is a serious matter that so many
are.

But yet there would not be a problem of the same kind
if only four rather than four million were unable to find
jobs. The abuse of the appeal to numbers should not obscure
the fact that to a very great extent it is the numbers
which constitute the problem. Finding useful and satisfying
employment for just one person is not an adequate or even
a very meaningful response to it. If we are to choose between
different policies for job-creation then, all other things being
equal, we may not choose on any other basis than arithmetical
efficiency, just because all other things are equal.

However, not only are other things in general often not equal, they are particularly not equal in the Survival Lottery. There we must choose, not between saving this number or that number of lives, but between not saving life and not killing on the one hand, and saving life through killing on the other. As in the case of Jim and the Indians, it is the fact that one course of action involves a killing that causes uneasiness about deciding on numbers alone. The reply to this is that not saving someone's life when you could have done so is not morally better than actually killing. (On some versions of this argument, not saving life *is* killing.) So not saving the lives of two patients who are in need of organ transplants is no better, morally, than killing them, if the operations can be performed and organs are available (albeit still in use, as it were, in the live donor). So although obtaining the necessary organs does involve killing someone, not obtaining them involves a course of action which is no better than killing two people. Whatever is done, someone is killed, or as good as killed. Therefore all other things *are* equal, and the issue must be decided on numbers alone. Killing the live donor in order to save the lives of at least two patients in need of transplants results in a net gain in lives of at least one, so that must be the preferred course of action.

This reply is seldom convincing, even to people who can see nothing wrong with it on grounds of logic. If this is not pure prejudice, then the problem must be more complicated than it has been made to seem. Can there be any justification for most people's deep-seated conviction that it cannot be right to save two lives at the cost of killing one? It cannot be that killing someone is always a worse thing to do than allowing them to die, for we saw in the preceding chapter that this is not so. However, we also saw that not saving someone's life is not always the same, not always as bad, as killing them. Not prolonging the life of someone who was dying, when there is good reason not to prolong their life, is not the same as killing them. This does not apply here, however. It is not true that either of those in need of transplants need necessarily die. (Nor is it true that the potential donor need necessarily die, though of course it cannot be that all three can live.) If the potential donor were already clinically dead (irreversible loss of higher brain functions), then her organs could be used. If she were close to death, then her dying need not be prolonged if she did not wish it, or was in no state to have any such wishes. Even here, however, it would not be permissible to kill her sooner than she would otherwise have died, even though she is going to die anyway.

This makes the difference appear highly marginal. If a patient is terminally ill but some of her organs may save the lives of other patients, it may be permissible to cease to use extraordinary means of treatment, particularly if she does not want them used or else has irrecoverably lost consciousness. The result may well be that her organs are available in time to save other patients. Why, then, if she is going to die, and quite soon, might she not be killed if that is the only way for the transplant operations to be performed in time for the recipients of the organs to benefit from them? The difference appears less marginal in a slightly modified version of the case.[14] Would it be permissible to kill a prisoner condemned to death a day before the execution date in order to provide urgently needed spare organs that will save the lives of two or more patients? Clearly most people would think not, even if it would be justifiable to take the organs after the execution.

It does not seem plausible to argue that the prisoner's last day is more valuable than the whole of the rest of two lives (though it is extremely valuable, none the less). The point seems rather that that last day is the *prisoner's* and no one may deprive her of it without the due process of the judicial system. Could we not, therefore, justifiably change the law so that the due process of law would permit this (given safeguards about appeals, etc.)? Again, it is likely that many people would object to that. What seems to be emerging, a little dimly, is the idea that it is *using* someone's death to benefit another which is suspect. Executing a condemned prisoner is justifiable if capital punishment is justified, because the punishment is addressed to the one who, it is claimed, merits it. Killing such a person for reasons which had nothing to do with the grounds for that punishment would be wrong. We might even feel that the public executioner, if she had private reasons for wanting the condemned prisoner dead, should not perform the execution. This is not an illogical feeling, though it might be a pointless one. (The above is not meant as an argument *for* capital punishment. What we have said is quite independent of the merits, or otherwise, of that case.)

By a parallel argument we might show that ceasing to treat a dying patient in order to benefit another, and not for reasons to do with the good of the patient, is to *use* that patient's death to benefit another, and is wrong if using the prisoner's death in that way is also wrong. Is it wrong? It has been argued that we *need* not sacrifice a life in order to save lives.[15] There is nothing wrong, it is claimed, in ignoring the appeal to greater numbers of lives saved and, though we may have a moral obligation to save life, we do not have a moral obligation to save the *maximum* number of lives possible. What this means in the case of the Scarce Drug problem, say, is that we may choose to save one rather than five, without wronging the five in any way. This is because none of them individually suffers anything worse than what we would inflict on the one if we passed her over in favour of the five. (Because each of the five suffers only one death; no one suffers five deaths.)

There is something in this, but it does not seem enough to justify the conclusion that numbers of lives saved never count, or need never be counted. Certainly we cannot add deaths together in any simple way. The five are not a composite entity which suffers five times as much as the one does.[16] But it does not follow from this that five deaths are not morally worse than one.

There are indeed circumstances in which numbers do not count with us. There may, in other words, be occasions on which it is *excusable* to save one rather than many. If a parent must choose between rescuing her own child and rescuing three other children, then she has an excuse if she rescues her own first. We would not suppose that she might then, if it were still possible to rescue the other three, say 'No. I need not. I have discharged my basic moral duties in saving *my* child.' She has an *excuse* if she saves her child because we would expect parents to attach great moral and emotional weight to the safety of their own children. In normal circumstances this emotional attachment ensures a morally beneficial outcome and we do not think it can easily be discounted or switched off on the rare occasions when the circumstances are not normal. This might be called 'guiltless wrong-doing'. But it *is* wrong-doing and the parent who behaves in this way is *excused* not exonerated.[17]

But this does not show that the numbers do not count. It shows that there are occasions when others might understand our disregarding them and treat us indulgently. It is not therefore a counter-example to the general principle that one is obliged to save more lives rather than less when one can. Still less can it justify our reluctance to kill in order to save life.

3   COLLECTIVISM AND INDIVIDUALISM

A more promising line to take could pick up the point raised in the previous section about using people to benefit others. Standardly this involves the notion of a right as a defence against external demands or pressures. The most straightforward way of presenting this case is to argue that no one is entitled to take anything from you unless you have consented to give it as a gift or in exchange for something else.

The strength of putting the case in this way is that violating someone's rights is not appropriately justified by appealing to the numbers of rights that are thereby not violated. This is especially the case where the rights are not equivalent, as in the Survival Lottery where the potential donor's right to life is not equivalent to the potential recipients' rights to treatment. For we do not violate their rights by not giving them the donor's organs; if the donor has the right to keep her vital organs then the recipients *have* no right to take them. It is also true that rights are not, properly, goods to be distributed at all; respecting them is a constraint on what distributions may be counted as just ones. If we violate the donor's rights, then we must, in justice, compensate *her*. So we may not kill her, even to protect the lives of others.[18]

This explains the intuition that no one may be killed in order to benefit another; but it does so at a cost. It commits its adherents to the view that no one may be compelled to give up *anything* to benefit another, unless they agree to give it up. There are, on this view, *no* social rights or entitlements. The only rights properly so-called are property rights: that is, rights to do what one chooses with whatever property one has justly acquired. This probably explains our view of what should happen in the Scarce Drug case when someone actually owns the drug they need to survive (see p. 174 above). But it also determines what should happen in other versions of the case. For it never happens that the drug does not belong to anyone. Thus, whoever owns it justly, may determine to whom it goes, and no injustice is done to anyone thereby. The general problem of health care resource allocation is to be treated in a similar way. The problem arises in its present form because it is assumed that no one has a claim to the resources prior to whatever distribution is fixed on. This, according to this view, is not the case. The resources are generated either by general taxation, or through the labour of health workers or both, and those resources should be returned to the tax-payers and the health workers who are their legitimate owners. They and they alone may determine what is to happen to those resources, on an individual basis. If the tax-payers would prefer to keep their taxes rather than pay them to the state, or the health workers to sell the fruits of their labours to the highest bidder, then they may, and no one may justly interfere with their decision to do so.

We have, then, two opposed and apparently mutually inconsistent and exhaustive positions on the issue of resource allocation. These generate two contrary and equally unattractive positions on the question of choosing between lives. The first, which has been exemplified by the Survival Lottery, is maximalist and collectivist. Health care resources are to be distributed on the basis of numbers of lives saved by a particular policy or institution. In deciding between policies individual lives are subordinated to the totality in the sense that any individual or individuals may be sacrificed if the consequence is that the total number of lives saved is greater than any alternative policy would have saved. Lives are to be saved at any cost, even that of lives.

The second, rights-based, view does not yield an *absolute* ban on killing, but something very close to it. Depriving someone of life may be justified if it prevents their taking yours. A right of self-defence exists, in other words, which may justify taking life if no other means exist of warding off a threat to life. Nothing else justifies the taking of life (though it may be given away), because nothing else justifies the taking of *anything* which belongs to someone else.

The first view, therefore, commits us to saving lives wherever we can, but compels us to kill if this is necessary to save (greater numbers of) lives. The second view forbids killing but also forbids any other kind of compulsory redistribution of goods. The first jettisons justice in favour of general welfare; the second jettisons welfare in favour of strict justice. The first gives the individual no rights to resist the demands of the collective; the second gives the individual a complete right to resist any demands made by the collective.

In the face of these two theories the temptation is to combine what is right about each – the obligation to save life from the first together with the obligation not to kill from the second. It would then follow that it is permissible to let someone die because the resources necessary to save them are needed to save more lives: and it is not permissible to kill someone in order to provide or release the resources which would save more lives elsewhere. This would be the conclusion most people's intuitions would support. But it hangs on just the thing rejected in the last chapter, namely, the existence of a distinction of moral significance between killing and letting die.

It has been suggested that what supports these intuitions is not the distinction beween killing and letting die, but something else.[19] Given equal harms it is better to save many from harm rather than a few, but where the harms are unequal we may not distribute them in a way which leaves someone worse off than everyone else. Suppose we must choose between saving one million people from a tax increase of £1 each or saving one person from bearing a loss equivalent to £750,000. Less money is lost overall if we let that loss fall on the individual (whom, we may suppose, will thereby be bankrupted, but saved from starvation by the social security system); but it would be more just to allow the loss to fall on the one million. The total loss is greater but no individual is made worse off than the others and so no injustice has been done.

The principle we appeal to if we decide in this way may be called the *maximin principle* – it maximizes the distribution of harms. This is clearly a more sophisticated principle than the simple maximization principle for the latter takes account only of total harms and benefits and not of how they are to be distributed. On the other hand, the maximin principle avoids commitment to the view that numbers do not count at all, a view which we have already seen is not very plausible. It is not, for example, a consequence of the maximin principle that we have to let one million people suffer a loss of £750,000 each in order to avoid taking £1 from someone who justly owns it. Where the harms are equal we save as many people from them as possible. But we owe a special duty to help those who are made the worst off by some distribution whether natural or social.

The maximin principle is more plausible than either the maximization principle or the rights-based theory because it recognizes, without exaggerating, the fact that justice in distribution has a geometry as well as an arithmetic.[20]

Some distribution patterns are to be preferred even though the total amount distributed is the same. Suppose we have a cake to be divided between ten people. The total distributed will be the same whether we give the whole cake to one person or an equal share to each of the ten. Other things being equal, justice tells in favour of equality rather than totality of distribution here. The maximalist might argue that it is not equality in itself which is important, but that giving everyone an equal share increases the total amount of happiness. To give anyone all of it would make them sick and the rest hungry and that way there is no happiness at all. But this need not be the case. If Billy Bunter were the one to whom we gave the whole cake that might well give him ten times as much pleasure as an equal slice would give everyone else. He might also get some dubious satisfaction from watching the envious expressions on everyone else's face whilst stuffing his own. Even if this were so, few would think that the just thing to do would be to distribute the pleasure (and the cake) unequally. And the same is true of the distribution of pain.

However, the maximin principle still does not give us a complete answer to our problem. Why, if in the case of the Scarce Drug problem it is permissible to save five at a cost of not saving one, is it not permissible in the case of the Survival Lottery to save two (or more) at the cost of killing one? The Survival Lottery obviously redistributes harms so that the total cost falls on just one – the donor – who is killed in order to benefit the others. This is a violation of maximin. However, distributing the scarce drug so that it saves five but lets one die, also lets the cost fall on just one in a way that makes her the worst off. But it does *not* seem objectionable to do this, in the same way that it does seem objectionable to kill in order to provide spare transplant organs. So again the only thing that seems to distinguish these two cases is that one involves killing and the other involves not saving a life.

What does distinguish the two cases is the difference of intention. In redistributing the scarce drug so that five live and one dies, we see but do not intend that the one will die. It is no part of our plan that the one should die; we would not, for example, have to murder her painlessly should she have a spontaneous remission from her illness and not need the drug after all. But in the Survival Lottery we cannot remove *vital* organs without necessarily killing the donor. The donor's death is connected logically, not just as a matter of fact, with what we intend to do to her in a way which makes it impossible to claim that her death is not any necessary part of our plan.

Given that the consequence of both plans is the same, this may seem an over nice point.[21] But it does seem to be an objection to some actions that they do not merely foreseeably cause harm to someone, but were intended to cause that harm in order that some other person may be benefited. It is clear that to offer someone an incompletely tested drug with known side-effects which may cause harm is permissible if there is a chance of benefiting the patient, and if the consequences of not benefiting her are sufficiently grave. It is not permissible to treat someone in this way in the hope, not of benefiting *her*, but of benefiting other patients who may in the future be treated with the drug. This is so, even if the harm risked or actually caused is notionally outweighed by the benefits of knowing more clearly what the harmful side-effects actually are. More clearly still, I may dash under a bus to rescue an errant child and sacrifice my life in doing so. I may not push you under the bus to achieve the same end. From the point of view of numbers this is totally inexplicable since the sums come out the same whichever is chosen.

It is almost certainly true that we could not avert all the harms that might befall people and it may be that in many cases we do not even have a strict obligation to try. Some things are truly none of our business; in some areas intervening may do more harm than good and, up to a point, we have a right not to jeopardize our own plans and projects for the sake of others. For the rest we almost certainly must do all we can. What we may not do is to deliberately incur harm for some in order to benefit others.

So we probably do owe Y and Z, the unfortunates who, in the Survival Lottery, are in need of vital organ transplants, everything we can reasonably do, through state-funded health care, by way of life-saving treatment. We cannot reasonably deliberately incur harm to A – the potential donor – in order to benefit Y and Z. Not treating someone – in say the Scarce Drug example – is not deliberately to harm them. It is not deliberate because we do not *choose* the harm; we simply cannot avoid it. In the Survival Lottery we *do* choose the harm; the harm is a necessary condition of benefiting Y and Z with the transplants they need.

No one has a right to life-saving treatment if others, because there are more of them, have a prior right to it. No one can rightfully demand what cannot, for quite legitimate reasons, be given to them. Equally Y and Z, even though there are more of them, cannot demand of A that she give up her vital organs for their benefit because she has a prior right to them which they may not violate. She has this right, not through ownership, but through something more fundamental. Property rights, though important in their way, are not basic. They are instrumental. We value property rights, and enshrine them in law, because they are a means of protecting certain other things we value, like a certain degree of material well-being, a degree of political and intellectual liberty, non-interference and privacy, etc. Where those more basic values are actually threatened by property rights, as in a free-market economy they might be threatened by the emergence of monopolies or other soures of potential economic coercion, etc., we place restrictions on property rights in order to safeguard the more basic values.

So A has no right to hang on to all her property and to refuse to pay taxes to support health care for those who need it. Threatening to deprive A of her life, as Y and Z do, is not to threaten to deprive A of something she would rather keep, but could manage without; it is to threaten A's very existence. A's life is not something she *owns* but a condition of her owning anything.

4   CONCLUSION

Oddly enough, the adherents of both the maximizing principle and the rights-based theory appear to have made the same mistake. They have assumed that one's body *is* something one owns. They then look for a general principle to defend or rebut the suggestions that we may take away what someone owns in order to benefit someone else. The maximizer finds a defence for the suggestion in the principle that goods are to be allocated where they do most good. (And in many circumstances, this is an eminently defensible principle.) So it seems to the maximizer that bodies, or bits of bodies, may be redistributed if this causes a net gain of good over bad (lives saved over lives lost). To the rights-based theorist this conclusion is so abhorrent that it then seems plausible to argue that no goods may be redistributed without the owner's consent, no matter what the beneficial consequences of so doing. The maximizer therefore becomes committed to the view that people's lives are *not* more important than the goods they own, and the rights-based theorist to the view that those goods are *just as* important as their lives. Here is an example of how that latter argument goes:

> May all entitlements be relegated to relatively superficial levels? For example, people's entitlements to parts of their own bodies? An application of the principle of maximizing the position of those worst off might well involve forceable redistribution of bodily parts ('You've been sighted for all these years; now one – or even both – of your eyes is to be transplanted to others'), or killing some people early to use their bodies in order to provide material necessary to save the lives of those who otherwise would die young.[22]

The author clearly thinks that 'forcible redistribution of bodily parts' is so obviously wrong that it grounds the belief that the forcible redistribution of anything must be wrong. To the maximizer the forcible redistribution of scarce goods in times of need is so obviously right that it even grounds the belief that 'bodily parts' may be forcibly redistributed.

The truth is, as in so many things, complicatedly somewhere in between. Your right to the things you own is not absolute; it can legitimately be overridden in all sorts of cases, but primarily in those cases where the need for them is much greater in others than in you. (There are all sorts of qualifications to that, but since they basically concern *how* these things may be taken from you, and not *whether* they may be, we will not go into them here.) But your body is not something you own along with your clothes, your books and your house. You *acquired* those things, and so it may be asked whether you acquired them justly, and whether your acquisition can be revoked or terminated. You did not acquire your body, since without it you do not exist (not in *this* world, at any rate), and equally you cannot dispose of it. You cannot give it away or sell it since it either remains yours or else you disappear altogether. And once you disappear, your body becomes a radically different kind of thing from what it once was. You *are* your body, you do not own it.

If this is right, then it follows that whatever your rights over your property, these are going to be quite different from the rights you have over your own body. This is recognized in most legal jurisdictions in the fact that rights over one's own body are *inalienable*, one cannot, for the most part, give them up, even willingly. You cannot sell your body during your own lifetime, you cannot consent to have it harmed except in special circumstances like surgery, and even if you yourself try to harm it, you may be certified insane and locked up. It therefore does not follow from the special status we give to rights of bodily integrity and self-determination, that we must grant the same status to rights of material ownership. Equally, it does not follow that not giving that special status to rights of material ownership means that we may not grant it to rights of bodily integrity.

People are not just objects to be shuffled around in a redistributive scheme. They are centres of consciousness and choice. If nothing had consciousness and nothing could choose, it is hard to see how anything could have value, for to say of something that it is valuable is to say that there are reasons for choosing it (though not to say that it is or ever has been chosen by anyone). To kill a human being is, then, a special wrong, not at all akin to obliterating any number of valuable *things*; for in killing a human being one is not destroying something of value, but a source of value.

If morality is to mean anything it must be concerned with people as moral agents acting within a world for whose state at any given time they are at least partially responsible. This is, in part, what is meant by saying that human beings are sources of value. To treat people's bodies as goods or resources to be redistributed as necessary in the furtherance of some desirable social or political end is to deny them their status as agents and to treat them as objects. Respecting their status as agents may well involve respecting their wish to cease to act, to cease to be objects and to withdraw from the world. There will, however, be certain constraints on what we can do to or for them based on the inalienability of their rights of bodily integrity and self-determination. We may do what we can to ease their deaths and even not intervene in their suicides. We may even, in extreme circumstances, provide them with what they need to die, though this will be exceptional and impermissible except where we cannot help them in any other way. What we must not do is to treat them as goods to be utilized for the benefit or convenience of other agents, to seek to end their lives on grounds which have nothing to do with their own good.

NOTES

1 Boyd, K. M. (1979) *The Ethics of Resource Allocation in Health Care*, Edinburgh University Press, p. 4.
2 *Ibid.*, p. 75.
3 Townsend, Peter and Davidson, Nick (1982) *Inequalities in Health: The Black Report*, Penguin, p. 29.
4 See Foot, P., 'The Problem of Abortion and the Doctrine of Double Effect', in Foot (1978), *op. cit.*, p. 24; also Locke, *op. cit.*, p. 453, and Taurek, J. (1977) 'Should the Numbers Count?', *Philosophy and Public Affairs*, 6, no. 4.
5 Lee, Robert (1986) 'The Legal Control of Health Care Allocation', University of Lancaster (unpublished ms.).
6 Excerpt of a group discussion on the comparison of need, reported by Boyd, *op. cit.*, p. 101.
7 See Hurthouse, *op. cit.*, pp. 143–4.
8 Anscombe, G. E. M. (1967) 'Who is Wronged?', *Oxford Review*, 5.
9 The *Montreal Gazette*, 27 July 1978. I am grateful to Martin Hollis for drawing my attention to this case.
10 See Glover, *op. cit.*, pp. 208–29; Harris, J. (1980) *Violence and Responsibility*, Routledge & Kegan Paul, pp. 71–2.
11 Smart, J. J. C. and Williams, B. (1973) *Utilitarianism: For and Against*, Cambridge University Press, p. 98.
12 Singer, Peter (1977) 'Utility and the Survival Lottery', *Philosophy*, 52, p. 218.
13 Harris, John (1975) 'The Survival Lottery', *Philosophy*, 50.
14 See Locke, *op. cit.*, pp. 457 and 474.
15 Taurek, *op. cit.*
16 Parfit, D. (1978) 'Innumerate Ethics', *Philosophy and Public Affairs*, 7, no. 4, pp. 294–5.

17 See Parfit, D. (1984) *Reasons and Persons*, Oxford University Press, Chapter 1, section 14.

18 See Nozick, Robert (1972) *Anarchy, State and Utopia*, Blackwell, esp. p. 206, for an argued account of this approach.

19 Parfit (1978), *op. cit.*, p. 296; Parfit cites Rawls, John (1974) 'Some Reasons for the Maximin Criterion', *American Economic Review*, 64, p. 142.

20 This metaphor, though not the way it is applied, is due to Holland, R. F., 'Absolute Ethics, Mathematics and the Impossibility of Politics', in Vesey, G. (ed.) (1978) *Human Values*, Harvester.

21 Though not so fine a distinction in other cases, which is why it matters. The ethics of testing drugs on human patients can be crucially affected by whether one foresees harm is possible and decides to risk it for the sake of the benefits, or whether one decides to inflict harm *in order to* secure benefits (toxicity testing, for example).

22 Nozick, *op. cit.*, p. 206.

Index

Index by Justyn Balinski